Little
Visits
with God

Little Visits® with God

Little Visits® Library Volume 4

Allan Hart Jahsmann and Martin P. Simon
Illustrated by Hal Lund

CPH™
SAINT LOUIS

Contents

Foreword

Here, indeed, is a unique book of devotions for families with young children. While involving their interest and participation, it also offers rich instruction for older children and adults.

There is nothing routine and formal about these devotions. They are full of warmth, dipped right out of life. Those of us whose children are grown could almost wish them young again in order to share these readings with them.

This book will help children not only to know about God but also to love Him and to trust in Him. It cultivates right attitudes and shows how the Christian faith is to function in daily living. These devotions touch the heart as well as reach the mind. They are childlike without being childish. They lead to Jesus, the Savior and Good Shepherd. And it is through childlike trust in Jesus that we are saved.

The authors are to be congratulated on their achievement, rarely equaled in the devotional literature I have seen. The church has produced many prayer books for small children. This is one of the first devotional books to capture the interest of the child along with the parent and to relate this interest to a discussion of the truths of Christian faith and life.

The authors represent a fine combination of talents united in a common task. Martin P. Simon, former editor of *The Christian Parent* magazine, was known for his ability to draw illustrations from everyday life. Allan Hart Jahsmann is a specialist in Sunday school materials for small children. He is the author of *Teaching Little Amalee Jane* and knows her brother Johnny, too.

It is a distinct pleasure to help send this book on its way into the hearts and homes of Christian parents and into the lives of their children. By using these devotions early in life, parents will sow seeds that will enrich all the years to come. Worship periods in the home produce God-fearing people who are also a blessing to others. May the church have many families who meet with God daily in family worship.

OSCAR E. FEUCHT

Authors' Note

The language used in these devotions was determined largely by a concern for the child. This accounts for the frequent use of popular, though sometimes "incorrect," grammar and the simplification of some of the Bible verses. Brief life-experience stories have been related to make the devotional readings more interesting and meaningful. You can provide a happy learning situation by taking time to visit with God as a family—either at the breakfast or supper table or at the child's bedtime. Older children will enjoy reading this book personally. The discussion questions are for informal conversation, and a hymn may precede or follow the reading. May the Holy Trinity be pleased with the book, and may all who use it be enriched as they commune with God and learn to follow their Savior, Jesus, more faithfully every day in every way.

A. H. J.   M. P. S.

Little Visits® with God

⌒

Blessed is he whose transgressions are forgiven. Psalm 32:1

Why We Can Always Be Happy

Jeremy wasn't happy. When his dad came home from work, Jeremy hurried upstairs. Mom had to call him four times before he came down to supper.

At the table, Dad asked, "Who broke the window in the garage?" Jeremy said nothing, but he felt his face get hot. "You played ball over there, didn't you?" said Dad. "And we told you not to."

Jeremy looked at his plate and still said nothing. He could hardly swallow the bread he was chewing. Then he began to cry.

"I'm sorry," he said. "I'll pay for it from my allowance. And I won't play ball there again. I promise."

His parents were glad to hear Jeremy talk that way. He was sorry he had done wrong. And he promised to do better.

"All right, Jeremy," said Dad softly. "We'll forget it. God forgives you every day because He loves you. And we forgive you, too, because we love you. But please don't disobey us again."

Next morning Jeremy whistled as he rode to school. He was happy now. God had put joy in his heart. I wonder why it feels so good to be forgiven, he thought.

"Thank You, God," he said, "for always being willing to forgive me."

~

Let's talk: Why didn't Jeremy want to see his dad? What had Jeremy done wrong? Was it easy for Jeremy to say, "I'm sorry"? Why did Jeremy feel so good the next day? The Bible says "Be glad in the Lord ... and shout for joy" because God forgives our sins every day for Jesus' sake.

Let's pray: Dear Lord, we're glad that we can come to You at any time and receive forgiveness. Keep us from doing wrong, make us sorry for our sins, and keep us as Your happy children because we believe in Jesus, our Savior. We ask this in Jesus' name. Amen.

In the beginning God created the heavens and the earth.
Genesis 1:1

What God Made

"My new bike is scratched," Jordan said. "I'll wait a few days; maybe it will get better." Will that bike get fixed? Not by itself.

"My hand is scratched," Ashley said. "I'll put on a Band-Aid; soon it will be better." Will that hand get better by itself? Yes, it probably will.

What's the difference? A human person made the bike. God created the hand. The things God created are much more wonderful than anything a human being can make.

What did God create? The Bible says that, in the beginning, all things in the world were created by Him. God created the sun and the moon and the stars. He created the lions and the cows. He created grass and trees and made them begin to grow. He created the first people.

"God saw all that He had made, and it was very good," says the Bible. What do you think of that?

When the world was created, God told the first people, "You take care of the world and rule it." He had put many wonderful things into the world for people to use to make things. He also gave people minds so they could figure out how to make things.

But in the very beginning, all things were created by God. And the things that God created still can't be made by people. You see, God is much wiser and greater than the people He created.

Let's talk: Why can a hand fix itself while a bike cannot? What are some things God created? For whom did He create them? What did He give to people so that they could make things from what He had created? What must God be if He created everything in the world?

Older children and adults may read: Genesis 1:1–31

Let's pray: What a wonderful world You have created for us, Lord. All that You have created shows Your great power and love. We're glad that You created us and that You also saved us when we became spoiled by sin. Give us your Holy Spirit so that we may all be and remain Your children. In Jesus' name. Amen.

Though you have not seen [Jesus], you love Him. 1 Peter 1:8

Not Seen, but Loved

"Mother, what does Jesus look like?" asked Shanika. Her aunt had given her a picture of Jesus for her birthday, and it didn't look like other pictures of Jesus at all.

Her mother couldn't tell her. "I don't know, honey," Mother said. "And nobody else knows either. Nobody made a picture of Jesus when He lived on earth. The pictures we see are just the way some painters thought He may have looked."

"You mean all the pictures are just pretend pictures of Jesus?" asked Shanika.

"That's right," said Mother. "Nobody really knows what Jesus looked like. Do you think you can still love Him even if you don't know what He looked like?"

"Oh, sure," answered Shanika. "I love Him no matter how He looks. I'd just like to know."

"Your question reminded me of a Bible verse," said Shanika's mother. "The verse says, 'Though you have not seen Jesus, you love Him.' That's what Peter wrote to all of God's children long ago."

"You know why, Mother? Because we know what He did for us," said Shanika. "That's why we love Him without knowing what He looks like."

Let's talk: What did Shanika want to know about Jesus? What do you think Jesus looks like? Who does Jesus look like? Why doesn't anybody really know? Why do we love Jesus even though we have never seen Him?

Older children and adults may read: 1 Peter 1:3–9

Let's pray: We would love You, dear Jesus, no matter how

You looked. We love You because You loved us and died on a cross to save us. Keep us from sin and take us to heaven, where we will see You and be with You forever. In Your name. Amen.

Serve the Lord with gladness! Psalm 100:2 (RSV)

Service with a Smile

"What's Elena doing?" asked her dad.

"She's helping Mom," said Cody.

Dad went to the kitchen to see how Elena was helping. She wasn't helping very much. She had a face a mile long, and it was sour enough to make pickles.

"Something must be wrong," Dad observed. "You don't look very happy helping your mother."

"No," said Elena, with a quiver in her voice.

"Okay," said Dad, "I'll finish drying the dishes for you if you'll learn a Bible verse for me."

Elena thought for a moment and figured it was a pretty fair trade. "What Bible verse?" asked Elena as her dad finished drying the dishes.

"It's in Psalm 100," said Dad. "Go get the Bible from the table and look up verse 2. The book of Psalms is easy to find—it's in the middle of the Bible."

Elena found it and read, "Serve the Lord with gladness."

"How are we to serve the Lord?" asked Dad, as though he didn't know.

"With gladness," said Elena. Then she thought a moment and asked, "Do I serve the Lord when I help Mom?"

"Yes," said Dad. "But I'm afraid you weren't doing it with gladness this time."

"I'm sorry," said Elena. "Next time I'll try to smile. I want Jesus to be happy with what I do."

Let's talk: What was Elena doing? How did she show that she wasn't glad to do it? Who finished her job for her? What Bible verse did Dad ask her to learn? Why did Elena want to serve the Lord with gladness?

Older children and adults may read: Psalm 100

Let's pray: Dear Lord Jesus, we're glad that You are our God and Savior and that we are Your children. Please help us remember that we serve You whenever we serve those around us. Then our work will become more enjoyable, and we will do it with gladness. In Your name. Amen.

[God] cares for you. 1 Peter 5:7

Let God Do Your Worrying

Ramon was taking his first trip in an airplane. He was on his way to Grandma's with his father and mother. Ramon was looking out the window at the wing, and the clouds, and the ground far, far below.

"Mother," Ramon said, "that big wall of clouds is blocking our way. Where will we go?"

"Don't worry," said Mother.

Father said, "Let the pilot worry about that, Ramon. He's flown to Cincinnati before."

Everything turned out all right. By the time they reached the big bank of clouds, the airplane was high above it. Ramon looked out the window again, but now he couldn't see any ground below, only the clouds.

"Mother," said Ramon, "how does the pilot know where Cincinnati is when he can't see the ground? All that's below us are clouds, and I don't see any signs to tell him where to go. What if he makes a wrong turn?"

"The pilot knows what he's doing," said Mother. "Let him do the worrying."

Ramon was young and had never flown before, so he worried about a lot of things. Even adults worry about things. Some say, "I'm afraid we won't have enough money when we're old." Others say, "I don't see how we can pay our doctor bill," or "How am I going to do all my work?"

The Bible says, "God cares for you." This also means, "God worries for you." In a way, He is like the pilot of an airplane. God knows the way, and He'll get you there safely. He'll also take care of you on the way. So why worry? Let God do your worrying for you.

Let's talk: Why did Ramon worry on the airplane? What did his mother and father tell him? Why do adults worry sometimes? Who is willing to worry for us? Why? Memorize the Bible verse.

Older children and adults may read: Psalm 23

Let's pray: Dear Jesus, we thank You for being willing to do our worrying for us. Please forgive us when we don't trust You. Help us remember how much You love us so that we won't worry. In Your name. Amen.

I will praise You, O Lord ... I will sing of You among the peoples. Psalm 108:3

Singing Praises to God

Kylie was only three years old and she couldn't talk very clearly, but she was singing at the top of her voice, "Dedud love me, did I know, fo da Biba tell me toe."

Do you know what she was singing? It doesn't matter. She was singing praises to God, and He heard it and was happy.

"I will sing praises to the Lord," said King David in Psalm 108. Almost every Christian boy or girl sings praises to God too. Why? Because in the Bible, God has promised to love us and help us and keep us as His children for Jesus' sake. That makes us want to thank and praise God, doesn't it?

What's one of the best ways to praise the Lord? By singing songs. Songs that tell what God has done for us help us thank Him for His wonderful love.

How many songs about God do you know? At home, in Sunday school, in church, or anywhere else, do you sing songs to God with gladness? Do you praise God when you sing songs about Him, or do you just move your lips and make sounds?

While you're waiting for church to begin, turn to a hymn you like and memorize a verse. Learn another verse each time you're in church until you know it all from memory. Then you can sing it at home, on the way to school, or any time.

It's good to sing to the Lord and praise Him with singing. Those who know and love God say, "I will praise You, O Lord … I will sing of You among the peoples."

Let's talk: What was Kylie singing? Why was God happy? Who said, "I will sing praises to the Lord"? Why do God's children enjoy singing songs about Him? What songs about God do you know? How could you learn more songs? What song could you sing together right now?

Older children and adults may read: Psalm 108:1–5

Let's pray: Dear Lord, teach me to sing Your praises. In Jesus' name. Amen.

The earth is the Lord's, and everything in it. Psalm 24:1

What Do You Think You Own?

"It's mine, and you can't have it," Aneko said to Kami. They were playing dress-up. Aneko was wearing one of mother's old dresses. She was reaching for the hat that Kami wanted for her outfit.

"It's mine," said Kami. "It's mine as much as yours."

Their mother came in just as the two began to argue. "Whose hat did you say that was?" Mother asked.

The girls looked at each other and began to giggle. "It's yours, Mother," they said together.

"But didn't I hear you say that it was yours?" Mother asked, looking at Aneko.

"Oh, we were just saying that," shrugged Aneko.

Mother sat down on the floor next to the girls. "Do you know what this makes me think about?" she asked. "God gives us so many things: food to eat, clothes to wear, a house to live in, good health so that we can work and earn money, a mind that can think. He also gives us the wood and rubber and metal that cars and TVs and everything else is made from. But all things really belong to God."

Aneko nodded. "I know. People act as though things belong to them, just the way we were acting," she said. "But they really don't, do they? God gives us everything, right?"

"Yes, He does," said Mother. "The Bible says, 'The earth is the Lord's, and everything in it.' Nothing that we have really belongs to us. It belongs to God. He just lets us have things to use and enjoy for a while. And God wants us to use the things He gives us to help other people."

⌒

Let's talk: Whose hat did both girls want? Whose hat did they say it was? Why do people act as though things belong to them? How many things really belong to us? Why does God give us things? Memorize the Bible verse.

Older children and adults may read: Psalm 50:10–15

Let's pray: Dear Father in heaven, please help us remember that all things in heaven and on earth belong to You and that we really don't own anything. Make us willing to use what You give us in ways that please You. Keep us from becoming selfish and thinking that things belong to us. Make us thankful for Your gifts and willing to help other people with them. In Jesus' name. Amen.

Wash me, and I will be whiter than snow. Psalm 51:7

How to Get Clean Inside

"Did you wash your hands, Jamal?" Mom asked.

"Yeah," came the quick reply. But when Jamal showed his hands to his mom, she was a little suspicious of his answer.

"You didn't use soap, did you? And you didn't wash here and here and here," she pointed out. So Jamal had to wash his hands again. This time he scrubbed them with soap.

There's one way children can usually get clean the first time—when they let their parents wash them. When parents do the washing, the outside usually is spotless.

But even parents can't wash away the bad things their children think and say and do. Parents can't wash away their children's sins. Only God can do that. When He forgives our sins, He washes them all away. That is why King David said, "Wash me, and I will be whiter than snow."

When your mom or dad does laundry, he or she wants everything to be clean, especially the white clothes. White shirts and sheets with streaks and stains on them aren't clean and beautiful. When we sin, it's like a stain on a clean sheet.

God wants His children to be clean on the inside. And we want to be clean and white on the inside for God, even when our hands and clothes get dirty. Because Jesus died and rose for us, we are clean on the inside. When God forgives us, He washes us so that not even one speck of sin is left. Isn't that wonderful?

⌒

Let's talk: Who could have washed Jamal better than he washed himself? What can't Jamal's mother wash away? Who alone can wash us on the inside? When God washes away sins, how many are left? How does God wash away our sins?

Older children and adults may read: Psalm 51:1–7

Let's pray: Forgive us all our sins, dear God, so that we may be whiter than snow and holy in Your eyes. In Jesus' name we ask this. Amen.

Always [give] thanks to God the Father for everything.
Ephesians 5:20

Always Thank God!

"Go to school. Wash the dishes. Make my bed," Rachel grumbled.

"Rachel, you're always grumbling," her dad said.

"Well, what *should* I do?" grumbled Rachel again.

"Jesus wants us to be thankful for everything," said Dad.

"Always?" asked Rachel. "For everything?"

"That's what it says in the Bible," Dad answered. " 'Always give thanks to God the Father for everything.' "

"You mean I should thank God for having to wash the dishes and make my bed?" Rachel asked.

"There are people who never have dirty dishes because they don't have much to eat," Dad replied. "There are some people who never have to make their beds because they're too poor to have beds."

"So when I wash the dishes, I should thank God for the food that made the dishes dirty," Rachel said with a smile of understanding. "And when I make my bed, I should thank God for having a nice warm bed."

"That's right, honey," Dad said. "I hope you'll learn to 'always give thanks for everything.' When you're giving thanks, you don't have time to grumble."

Let's talk: Why did Rachel grumble and complain? What Bible verse did Dad teach her? What can we thank God for when we have dishes to wash? Why can we be thankful that we have a bed to make? Which person reflects Jesus' love—the thankful person or the one who whines? Which person is happier—the person who grumbles or the one who is thankful?

Older children and adults may read: Ephesians 5:17–21

Let's pray: Dear Father in heaven, help us remember how much You love us. Help us believe that all things are just right for those who love You. Help us live as your thankful children. We ask this in Jesus' name. Amen.

Be imitators of God, ... as dearly loved children. Ephesians 5:1

Following Our Leader

"Follow the leader!" cried the boys and girls at Jason's birthday party. Then Jason led everyone up into the attic and down into the basement and outside between the bushes and around the trees.

When the children came in for lunch, Jason's father said, "You're all very good at following the leader. I didn't think Christina would keep up with you.

"I know another way to play follow the leader," said Father.

"Let's play it," the children shouted.

"Maybe I shouldn't have said it was a game," Father added. "It's really about how we are to live our lives. As Christians, we're supposed to follow our Leader—God. When you were playing follow the leader, I remembered a Bible verse. It says 'Be imitators of God.' I wrote it on a card for each of you to take home."

Everybody looked at the cards by their plates. It had these words printed on it: "Be imitators of God."

"What's an imitator?" Christina asked.

"Remember when Jason led you around the yard and you had to walk like he did to avoid the mud," Father explained. "You had to imitate him or you would get dirty.

When we imitate God, we try to follow what Jesus said and did. Do you think you can do that?"

"No," said one of the boys, "sometimes it's hard to be good. But it's fun trying to imitate God when you love Jesus."

"You're right," said Jason's father. "And Jesus sends us the Holy Spirit to help us imitate Him. Do you know what Jesus wants His imitators to do? The Bible says, 'Love, just as Christ loved us.' We imitate our leader Jesus by loving."

Let's talk: What did the children play at Jason's party? Why was it hard to follow Jason? What verse did Jason's father write on cards for the children? What does Jesus want His followers to do?

Older children and adults may read: Ephesians 4:31–5:4

Let's pray: Dear Lord Jesus, we don't always imitate You as we should. Please forgive us. Send us Your Holy Spirit to help us imitate You. Help us to love others as You have loved us. In Your name. Amen.

The eyes of the Lord are everywhere. Proverbs 15:3

God Sees Everything

"I wish God didn't see everything," Daniel said. "Then He wouldn't see what I do wrong."

"I'm glad God sees everything," replied Kyle. "That's how He can help me all the time."

Both Daniel and Kyle had good reasons for what they said, but who do you think was right?

The Bible says, "The eyes of the Lord are everywhere." God sees the bad that we do and also the good. He knows what we're thinking and whether we believe in Him. The eyes of the Lord see in the dark as well as in the light. They see us all the time.

We're all like Daniel. We sin and wish God couldn't see it. But we can't hide from God; He is everywhere. And we can't hide what we do from Him because He sees everything.

There's only one way to hide our sins. God has to hide them. We know that God forgives our sins for Jesus' sake. And He doesn't just cover them up, He completely wipes them away. Because He forgives our sins, we never have to be afraid of Him. Instead, we can be glad that God sees us everywhere so that nothing can hurt us.

Let's talk: Where are the eyes of God? What does this mean? Why didn't Daniel like it? Why was Kyle happy that God's eyes are everywhere? What is the only way our sins can be hidden from God? Why don't we ever have to be afraid that God can see us? Why is it a good thing that the eyes of the Lord are everywhere? Memorize the Bible verse.

Older children and adults may read: Psalm 139:1–12

Let's pray: Dear Lord God, we know that we can't hide anything from You. You know the truth about us all the time. Please forgive all of our sins for Jesus' sake so that we don't have to be afraid of what You see. Then we can be happy that Your eyes are everywhere and are always watching over us. In Jesus' name. Amen.

Even the very hairs of your head are all numbered.
Matthew 10:30

God Counts Our Hairs

"How many children are there in the world, Daddy?" asked Luisa.

"I don't know," said her daddy. "Millions and millions of them, I guess."

"Then how can God take care of me?" asked Luisa.

"How can He know where I am and what's happening to me? There are so many other boys and girls."

"God knows about you all right," said Daddy. "He not only knows you, He knows how many hairs you have. And He knows when one of them falls out.

"How many sparrows do you think there are in the world?" Daddy asked.

Luisa thought for a moment. "More sparrows than children, I guess," she answered.

"Jesus said that God cares for every sparrow. Not even a sparrow can die without God knowing about it. So if God takes care of every sparrow, don't you think He can take care of you, too?" asked Daddy.

"Sure," said Luisa. "But I didn't know He counted my hairs."

"He doesn't have to count them like you or I would," Daddy explained. "He knows everything, and He knows how many hairs we have without counting them. In fact, He knows all about us and takes care of us because He loves us. Jesus said, 'Don't be afraid; you are worth more than many sparrows.' "

Let's talk: What did Luisa want to know? Why? What did Jesus say God knows about our hair? How well does God watch sparrows? Who is worth more to God than many sparrows? Memorize the Bible verse. Why did Jesus tell us these words?

Older children and adults may read: Matthew 10:29–39

Let's pray: We thank You, dear Father in heaven, for loving us and watching over us. Remind us that You know all about us at all times and nothing can happen unless You let it happen. Keep us from sin and every evil for Jesus' sake. Amen.

Children, obey your parents in everything. Colossians 3:20

How Jesus Obeyed for Us

Who was the only perfect boy who ever lived? It was Jesus. When His mother, Mary, asked Him to get some water for her, He did it gladly. When His earthly father, Joseph, who was a carpenter, needed someone to hold a board, Jesus did it gladly. Jesus didn't grumble. He didn't disobey. He probably even did things without being asked.

The Bible says Jesus *obeyed* His earthly parents.

But didn't Jesus ever play? Oh, yes. His parents gave Him time to play, and they had fun together with Him. They probably had a happy home in Nazareth. His parents were happy because Jesus obeyed them.

Jesus is God. God doesn't have to obey people. But Jesus had a special reason for obeying Mary and Joseph. He did all the things God wants *us* to do. Jesus did everything perfectly for us so we could be saved. Because of His example, we know that we should obey our parents in everything. When we love Jesus, we willingly obey our parents.

Let's talk: Who was the best boy who ever lived? How well did He obey His parents? Why didn't Jesus really have to obey His parents? Why did He want to obey them? How well does He want us to obey our parents? Why do we want to obey our parents? Memorize the Bible verse.

Older children and adults may read: Colossians 3:20–25

Let's pray: Dear Jesus, please forgive us for not always obeying our parents the way You obeyed Mary and Joseph. Send us Your Holy Spirit to help us become more like You and gladly do what our parents ask. In Your name. Amen.

Even a child is known by his actions. Proverbs 20:11

How Others Get to Know You

"That boy over there looks like a good boy," said Mr. Brandt to the check-out person at the grocery store.

"He does now, but let's watch him for a few minutes," replied the checker.

They watched the boy. He hit his mother because she wouldn't get the cereal he wanted. He stomped down the aisle toward the cookies. When his mother asked him to come back, he turned his back to her. A girl was in front of the cookies he wanted, so he pushed her out of the way.

"Watching that boy reminds me of the Bible verse, 'Even a child is known by his actions,' " said the checker.

"You can know what kind of person a child is by what he or she does. That boy isn't acting like a good boy. He doesn't obey his mother or treat others as he would like to be treated."

Jesus said "By their fruit you will recognize them." He meant that you will know a person from the things he says and does.

It's easy to say that we love Jesus. But people can tell whether we really love Him by the way we act. Even children are known by their actions. What does your behavior tell about you? Can others see that you're a Christian from the way you act? Those questions remind us to act as Jesus would. Then people will know that we belong to Him.

⏛

Let's talk: At first, what did Mr. Brandt think about the boy in the store? What changed his mind? What Bible verse did the check-out person tell Mr. Brandt? What did Jesus mean when He said you could know people by their fruits? If people, even children, say they are good, but they behave badly, are they good or bad? How can children show that they love Jesus?

Older children and adults may read: Proverbs 20:11–13

Let's pray: Dear God, we want others to know that we're Your children. We want to be witnesses for You so that others can see our good actions and learn about You. Please help us do what is right so that people will know that we love Jesus. Thank you for forgiving us when we do wrong. In Jesus' name. Amen.

Nothing is impossible with God. Luke 1:37

God Can Do Anything

One winter some enemy soldiers were entering a little town. A Christian mother sat in one of the houses near the town. She was praying.

"Dear God, please build a wall around us and protect us from the soldiers," she prayed.

Her son heard her. He didn't believe in God. He said, "Mother, your God can't build a wall around us in one night." But the mother kept praying.

The next morning, her son could hardly believe what he saw. He couldn't look out the windows.

"Come here, Mother," he called. "God sent a snowstorm, and the wind has blown a big wall of snow against the house."

Now the son believed that God could do anything and that He answers the prayers of His children. The soldiers had marched right past the house without even seeing it.

There isn't anything that can stop God from doing what He wants to do for us. Long ago God made the promise that He would send a Savior. He said the Savior would be His very own Son. When it was time for the Savior to come, Mary was chosen to be His mother. God's own Son became a baby. God did this to save us all from sin. "Nothing is impossible with God," says the Bible.

Let's talk: How many promises of God can you think of? What promises has He kept? What promises will God keep? When should God keep His promises: When He knows the time is right or when we think the time is right? What's the best way for God to answer our prayers: How we want them answered or the answer *He* knows is best?

Older children and adults may read: Luke 1:26–38

Let's pray: Dear God, thank You for the wonderful promises You have given us in the Bible. Thank You most of all for sending our Savior as You promised You would. We're glad that You can do anything and that You always keep Your promises. Help us trust You always, for Jesus' sake. Amen.

Love the Lord your God with all your heart ... and love your neighbor as yourself. Luke 10:27

A Man Who Was Helpful

A man was riding on a donkey down a dusty road. Suddenly some robbers jumped from behind a rock. They hit him over the head. The man fell off the donkey, and the robbers beat him. They took all his money and possessions. Then they ran away into the hills. They left the man lying next to the road. He was almost dead.

Two people who saw the injured man walked past him. They didn't want to help. Then a kind stranger came by. He felt sorry for the injured man. He stopped to help. He bandaged the man's wounds. He put the man on his own donkey and took him to a hotel. He even paid somebody to take care of the man until he got better.

When we need help, wouldn't we want some kind person to help us? If someone needs help, Jesus said we are to be good neighbors, like the one who helped the injured man in the story. We are to love our neighbors as we love ourselves. And we love our neighbors because Jesus first loved us.

Let's talk: What happened to the man in the hills? What did two people do when they passed by the injured man? What did the third man do? Which one loved his neighbor? Have you ever helped someone?

Older children and adults may read: Luke 10:30–37

Let's pray: Heavenly Father, please forgive us for doing so little for others. Show us how to be good helpers and make us glad to help. We ask this for Jesus' sake. Amen.

I was glad when they said to me, "Let us go to the house of the Lord." Psalm 122:1 (RSV)

Are You Glad to Go to Church?

"Do I *have* to go to Sunday school and church?" asked Garrett. His friends were going fishing, and they had asked him to go along. "Do I *have* to?"

"Yes, Garrett, you have to," said Dad. "But what will it take to make you say, 'I *want* to'?"

"But it's going to be a great day for fishing," said Garrett.

"It's also going to be a great day for hearing God's Word," said Dad. "Sunday is called the Lord's day. Every day belongs to Him, but Sunday is one day when Christians go to their church. Those who love Jesus more than anything else say what King David said long ago."

"What was that?" asked Garrett.

"He said, 'I was glad when they said to me, "Let us go to the house of the Lord." ' He wrote that in one of his psalms or songs of praise to God," explained Dad.

"You know what, Dad, I'm *glad* to go to church," said Garrett. "Only tomorrow, I'd like to go fishing."

"I know how you feel," said Dad. "It isn't that you don't want to go to church. I'm sure you'd be very unhappy if our church were closed and we didn't have any place to worship God. But what if everybody went fishing tomorrow? Do you think there would be a church service?"

"No, I guess not," said Garrett.

"What if we went fishing in the afternoon?" asked Dad.

"That would be great, Dad," said Garrett. He really did *want* to go to church because he loved Jesus. Now he was glad he could go fishing, too.

Let's talk: Where did Garrett want to go? Why did Dad say he *had* to go to church? What did King David say when he thought of going to church? What would Garrett have loved more than God if he had gone fishing instead of to church? What is more important, fishing or visiting with God in His house? Memorize the Bible verse.

Older children and adults may read: Luke 2:41–49

Let's pray: We know how much we need to hear and learn Your Word, dear God. Please help us to love it, understand it, remember it, and do it. Forgive us for not always loving You and Your house above all things. Help us to gladly go to Your house whenever we can. In Jesus' name. Amen.

Grow in the grace and knowledge of our Lord and Savior Jesus Christ. 2 Peter 3:18

Are You Growing as a Christian?

When Rosa was not quite two years old, people would ask her, "How big are you?" Rosa would raise her hands up high and say, "So big." Now that Rosa is grown up, she doesn't say that anymore.

When our bodies are as tall as they're meant to be, we say that we have stopped growing. But there are some ways in which we can keep growing. Peter, one of Jesus' disciples, says in our Bible verse, "Grow in the grace and knowledge of our Lord and Savior Jesus Christ."

What does it mean to "grow in grace"? What is grace, and how can we grow in it?

Grace is the wonderful love of God. Peter wants our faith in this love to grow and grow. To another group of

Christians the apostle Paul wrote, "We ... thank God ... your *faith* is growing more and more." *Faith* is believing that God loves us and that He forgives our sins and makes us His children. Peter wants us to learn to trust God's love more and more.

To grow in grace, we must grow in another way. We must learn to know Jesus better all the time. Only people who know Jesus know how good He is to them. That's why Peter also said we should grow in knowing our Lord.

Let's talk: When do people say they have stopped growing? What does our Bible verse tell us to keep growing in? What is grace? How can our faith in God's love keep on growing? In what ways can we learn more about Jesus?

Older children and adults may read: 2 Thessalonians 1:2–12

Let's pray: Dear Father in heaven, we want to keep on growing as Christians. Please help us grow in grace by leading us to learn more about Jesus, our Lord and Savior. In His name. Amen.

The Lord is near to all who call on Him. Psalm 145:18

Where God Is

It was a lot of fun to drive out to the mountains. The trip took Stephen and Ryan far away from home. First the boys counted cars. Then they raced to see who could count 100 cows on his side of the road first. Later they raced to be the first to see a white animal—a white horse or a cat or a cow or a dog. By evening, they were hundreds of miles from home.

That night as Stephen lay in a cabin in the woods, something popped into his head and stayed right there. The more he thought about it, the more worried he became.

"Mom, how can we pray to God?" Stephen asked. "He isn't way out here, is He?"

"Yes, He is, dear," Mom answered. "God is everywhere. We could drive all around the world, and God would still be there. There isn't a place where God is not. No matter where we are, God can hear our prayers."

"Is God nearby?" Ryan asked. "Can He hear if I just whisper my prayers?"

Mom smiled. "Yes, He can hear you," she answered. "You don't even have to whisper them. You can just think them, and God will hear your thoughts. The Bible says, 'The Lord is near to all who call on Him.' "

So Stephen and Ryan said their prayers and went happily to sleep.

Let's talk: Why did Stephen think that God couldn't hear his prayers? Where is God? How loud must a prayer be for God to hear it? According to the Bible verse, to whom is God very near? How can we call on the Lord? Memorize the Bible verse.

Older children and adults may read: Psalm 145:18–21

Let's pray: Thank You, dear Lord, for loving us and hearing our prayers no matter where we are. Please forgive us all our sins. Thank you for being with us always, when we're at home or when we're away. We pray this in Jesus' name because we belong to Him. Amen.

Ask and it will be given to you. Luke 11:9

Why Not Ask?

The apples on the tree in the neighbor's yard looked very good to Erin. But she knew that they didn't belong to her. "I wish I could have some of those apples," Erin told her dad.

"Why don't you ask Mrs. Harris if you may have one?" asked her dad.

"I don't know," said Erin. "I'm afraid to talk to her." Erin was very shy.

One day Mrs. Harris was walking past Erin's house. "Your apples look very pretty, Mrs. Harris," Erin said.

"Do they?" Mrs. Harris replied. "Would you like some?"

Erin nodded her head.

"Well, I'm glad you talked to me," said Mrs. Harris. "You may go and pick some any time, but don't waste them."

Erin didn't wait long. She hurried over to Mrs. Harris' yard to get some apples. She could have had them sooner if only she had asked for them.

Did you know that we could have many more good things if we asked God for them? Jesus said, "Ask and it will be given to you." Ask God for the things you need or would like. God listens when we pray, and God answers the prayers of His children. Don't be afraid to ask God for things. He loves us for Jesus' sake. He will give us whatever is good for us.

Let's talk: What did Erin wish she could have? What did Dad tell her to do? How did Mrs. Harris show that she liked Erin? Do you think God loves His children as much as Mrs. Harris liked Erin? Suppose we ask God for something He doesn't want us to have. How would God answer our prayer? What are some gifts that God is always willing to give us?

Older children and adults may read: Luke 11:5–10

Let's pray: Thank You, dear God, for telling us to ask You for whatever we want. Teach us to trust that You will give us what You know is best for us. We especially ask You for a strong faith in Jesus, our Savior, and for Your Holy Spirit to fill our hearts. We ask this in Jesus' name. Amen.

[God] sends lightning with the rain. Psalm 135:7

How Strong God Is!

One day James noticed how strong his dad was. When Mom couldn't open a jar of pickles, she called Dad. He opened it. A little later his brother, Robert, couldn't get the screen out of a window. But Dad got it out easily. Then the faucet leaked, and Dad fixed it.

The next day, James went next door to play with Christopher. "My dad is strong—he can do anything," James told Christopher. Did knowing his dad was strong make James afraid? No, it made him feel good.

When you hear thunder and see lightning, remember that God makes the thunder roll and the lightning crack. Remember, too, that God is your Father in heaven. Your heavenly Father sends the lightning with the rain, says the Bible.

The next time you see God's lightning and hear His thunder, think about how strong and great God is. James said his father could do "anything." James was wrong. Only our Father in heaven can do anything—anything He wants to do. And He wants to do only what is good for us. We're His children, and He loves us very much.

Do we ever have to be afraid of lightning? No. It shows us how strong and great our God is. Think of that when you see the lightning. And remember how wonderful it is that you are one of God's children.

⁓

Let's talk: When does God usually send lightning? Why are some people afraid of lightning? What does lightning tell us about God? Does God want to scare us with thunder and lightning? Can God keep the lightning from hurting us? How do we know that God loves us? What can we do if we become afraid in a thunderstorm?

Older children and adults may read: Psalm 135:5–7

Let's pray: Dear Father in heaven, only good things come from You, so lightning must be good for us. Whenever there's lightning, help us remember how strong You are and how happy it makes us that we are Your children. We ask this in Jesus' name. Amen.

Be on your guard against all kinds of greed. Luke 12:15

You Shall Not Covet

A man watched a zoo keeper feed a monkey. The zoo keeper put the monkey's food on the floor of the cage. The monkey was all alone, but it must have been afraid another animal would take some of the food. The monkey grabbed the food as fast as it could. It stuffed three bananas into its mouth and put an apple under each arm. Then the monkey grabbed a loaf of bread in one hand and a bunch of carrots in the other.

There was a big piece of lettuce left on the floor. The greedy monkey put down the carrots, picked up the lettuce, and put it on its head. Then the monkey picked up the carrots again and went to a corner of the cage. The monkey wanted all the food. It was selfish. But the monkey couldn't eat because its mouth was full of the food it was holding.

Jesus said, "Be on your guard against all kinds of greed." To be greedy, or to covet, means to be selfish, to want things for yourself.

To show how foolish and wrong it is to covet, Jesus told a story about a rich man who wanted to get richer. He kept building bigger and bigger barns so that he could keep more and more for himself. But he never thanked God, and he never helped others. When the selfish rich man wanted to start enjoying everything he had collected, God took his life away.

Jesus said a person's life does not depend on what things he or she has. Remember this the next time you think you must have something to be happy. Wanting things often makes people unhappy. The only thing we need to be happy is Jesus' love, and we have that all the time. That's why God's children can be unselfish.

Let's talk: How did the monkey show it was greedy and selfish? When does a person covet? What story did Jesus tell to show how foolish it is to covet? What is the only thing we need to be happy?

Older children and adults may read: Luke 12:15–21

Let's pray: Dear Lord Jesus, please teach us not to covet things or to be greedy. Give us those things we need and lead us to use Your gifts and blessings for the good of others. In Your name. Amen.

Do not merely listen to the Word … . Do what it says.
James 1:22

Practicing Your Lessons

Two girls were playing on the floor as their mother entertained some guests. Everyone was at the dinner table, ready to start eating.

Mother said to the girls, "Please come to the table. We're ready to eat." But the girls paid no attention to her, not even when she said it two more times.

One of the dinner guests was the girls' Sunday school teacher. She asked the girls, "I wonder which of you can finish this Bible verse: 'Children, obey …' "

Both girls quickly answered, "Children, obey your parents in the Lord, for this is right."

The verse told the girls to obey their mother, but they still *didn't* obey. What was wrong?

The girls were *hearers* of the Word of God but not *doers*. They knew the words, but they didn't *do* what the words said. Knowing the words didn't help the girls, did it? They needed to *do* what they had learned.

God wants us to put into practice the words of the Bible. The words won't change us and help us until we do what they say. The apostle James writes, "Do not merely listen to the word .... Do what it says."

The first thing God wants us to do is to believe in Jesus. When we believe in Jesus, we also want to obey Him.

⤳

Let's talk: What did Mother tell the girls? What did the girls do? How did their teacher try to help? What Bible verse did the girls know? Why didn't the words help? What is the first thing God wants us to do?

Older children and adults may read: James 1:22–25

Let's pray: Dear Lord God, we're thankful for Your wonderful words in the Bible. We want to hear and learn them. Help us not only to remember them but also to do what they say. Remind us that as we obey Your words, we show our love for Jesus, who died for us. In His name we pray. Amen.

Since God so loved us, we also ought to love one another.
1 John 4:11

The Way to Love Everyone

Shelly was very nice to people when she was in public. But at home she was often mean to her little brother. Shelly could be so kind to people at church, but she was not always kind to her mother.

Sometimes we can be difficult to get along with, especially at home. Sometimes we forget to do things. Sometimes we feel mean. But when we remember how kind and good Jesus is, we want to be kind and good also. And when we remember that Jesus died to save us, we find it easier to be friendly to other people. Loving Jesus makes us more like Him.

Jesus said, "Love your neighbor as yourself." He even told us to love our enemies. Jesus always loved. We often don't. But that's why He paid for our sins on the cross. "Since God so loved us, we also ought to love one another."

Don't you think your home is a good place to practice loving others? People could tell what kind of girl Shelly really was by the way she acted at home. If we love Jesus, we will want to be kind in public and especially in our home.

Let's talk: To whom was Shelly nice? To whom was she mean? Why should we show love, especially to those we live with? From whom can we learn to be kind? How did Jesus pay for our sins? What does our Bible verse say we should do because God loves us?

Older children and adults may read: 1 John 4:10–12

Let's pray: Dear God, we know that You love us even though we are not always loving to others. In fact, You loved everyone in the whole world when You sent Jesus to save us all. Help us love those around us and forgive us when we forget. We ask this for Jesus' sake. Amen.

[God] has made everything beautiful. Ecclesiastes 3:11

Why the World Is So Pretty

Mei Ling and her father were walking along a path near the river. At one spot Mei Ling saw some flowers she had never seen before. "Look how pretty those flowers are," exclaimed Mei Ling. "There are so many colors."

As they walked a little farther, Mei Ling saw some wild strawberries. She picked a few and showed them to her father. "Look how pretty these strawberries are," she said. "They're like a red ice-cream cone on green leaves."

Then Mei Ling noticed the round stones by the side of the river. They had been washed smooth by the water. She picked some up to take home. "Look how they shine," she said. "Red and yellow and lots of other colors all mixed up."

"Mei Ling, I'm glad you can see how beautiful God made things," said Father. "Just look at the river and those trees over there and that beautiful blue sky and the green grass all around. The Bible says, 'God has made everything beautiful.'"

"But if God made everything beautiful, why are some things not beautiful anymore?" asked Mei Ling.

"That's a good question," said Father. "Things have been spoiled by sin. People have spoiled things by doing wrong. But God sent His Son, Jesus, to take away all sin. Jesus came to straighten things out and make everything beautiful again."

On the way home Mei Ling didn't say much. She was thinking of how good it was that God had made everything beautiful.

Let's talk: What did Mei Ling notice as she and her father walked by the river? Why do you think God made the world beautiful? What do you think is especially beautiful in the world? What question bothered Mei Ling? Why are some things not beautiful? Who came to take away all sin and to make everything right and beautiful again?

Older children and adults may read: Matthew 6:28–30

Let's pray: Dear Father in heaven, thank You for making everything beautiful and just right. Forgive us for spoiling things, and make our lives beautiful through Jesus Christ, our beautiful Savior. In His name. Amen.

All that is within me, bless His holy name. Psalm 103:1 (RSV)

Thank God All You Can

When Kenji blew his whistle, it was loud and clear. But when he blew it with all his might, it was even louder.

When Kenji ran, he ran fast. But when he ran as fast as he could, he ran really fast. Whatever Kenji did with all his might, he really did well.

In Psalm 103, King David wrote about thanking and praising God. He wanted to remind himself to bless God with everything in him. "Praise the Lord, O my soul," he wrote, "all that is within me, bless His holy name."

How would Kenji praise God with everything in him? He would do it just as well as he could, with everything he's got. When King David wrote, "all that is within me, bless His holy name," he meant, "I want to thank God with everything in me."

When somebody gives Kenji a cookie, Kenji says, "Thank you." But when somebody gives Kenji ice cream covered with strawberries, he gets excited and says, "Thank you. Thank you very much. Thanks a lot!"

Some people thank God a little now and then for things He gives them. But those who remember how God forgives their sins and is good to them every day thank Him with everything that's in them.

⌒

Let's talk: When Kenji blew his whistle as loud as he could, how did it sound? When Kenji ran with all his might, did he run faster or slower? What did King David remind himself to do in our Bible verse? Why did King David want to praise God as much as he could? When we appreciate how much God loves us and provides for us, how will we praise and thank Him?

Older children and adults may read: Psalm 103:1–5

Let's pray: If we had a thousand voices, dear God, we would want to use them all in thanking and praising You. Thank You for sending Jesus to die for us. We praise You for being kind and good to us instead of punishing us as we deserve. Please forgive all our sins for Jesus' sake. Amen.

I am your God. ... I will ... help you. Isaiah 41:10

God's Business

Some children went to the zoo with their Uncle Mark. They saw the lions and the elephants and the monkeys and the camels.

All at once the children knew they were lost. They could not see Uncle Mark anywhere. They didn't know where the car was. They didn't know which way the gate was.

While looking around, they saw a sign that said, "Information." Courtney went up to the woman who sat below the sign. Everybody was asking her questions. Courtney didn't really want to bother her, but she had to. She said, "I wish I didn't have to ask you for help, but ..."

"Go ahead and ask," said the woman. "It's my business to help you. That's what I'm here for." She told the children which way to go, and soon they found Uncle Mark waiting for them by the gate.

Sometimes people think they shouldn't bother God with all their little troubles. They think God may have too many other things to do.

What do you think God would say to children who feel that they shouldn't tell Him about something that bothers them? In the Bible, God speaks to us the way the woman in the zoo spoke to Courtney. God says, "Go ahead and ask for help. I am your God. I will help you."

God wants to help us. He loves to do it. Nothing is too small for Him. Nothing is too big for Him. God says, "Don't worry. Don't ever be afraid. I am your God. I will help you."

Let's talk: Why didn't Courtney want to ask the woman for help? What did the woman say? In what way is our Father in heaven like the woman who helped Courtney? How big must a trouble be before we can ask God for help? How big can it be? Why is God willing to help us?

Older children and adults may read: Psalm 121

Let's pray: Thank You, dear Father in heaven, for promising to help us at all times. We don't deserve to have You as our God, but we're glad You are. Keep us as Your children for Jesus' sake. Amen.

[God] said to me, "My grace is sufficient for you ... "
2 Corinthians 12:9

Joseph and the Mouse

One day a mouse came to Joseph. The mouse was very worried. At first Joseph didn't see the mouse. He was busy figuring how much wheat he had left to feed all the people. He had mountains of wheat, much more than enough. Then he heard the mouse squeak.

"What are you worried about, Mouse?" asked Joseph.

"I'm worried that you won't have enough wheat for me," said the mouse.

Joseph laughed. There was enough wheat to last the mouse a million years or more.

That story was told by Mr. Spurgeon, a great preacher who lived in England. Mr. Spurgeon went on to say that one day he was worried about his troubles. He didn't think that everything would come out all right. Then he read the Bible and came to the verse where God says, "My grace is sufficient for you." That means God's love and grace is enough to help us with every problem.

When Mr. Spurgeon read those words, he laughed. He laughed at himself. He was being as foolish as the mouse that came to Joseph and worried that there wasn't enough wheat.

Do we ever have troubles? Yes, but none of our troubles are too big for God to handle. No matter how much trouble we may have, no matter what we need, God's grace and love can take care of us.

Remember what God said: "My grace is sufficient for you."

Let's talk: What was the mouse worried about? Why did Joseph laugh? That story isn't really true, but what does it teach us? Why did Mr. Spurgeon laugh as he read the Bible one day? Is God's grace big enough to take care of our troubles? To whom does God give His grace?

Older children and adults may read: 1 John 5:11–15

Let's pray: Dear God, we know that Your grace is big enough to take care of all our troubles. Forgive us when we don't trust You. Help us remember that all we need is Your grace. Please give us this for Jesus' sake. Amen.

Be kind and compassionate to one another. Ephesians 4:32

The Fun of Being Kind

"You didn't make your bed yet, Ross," scolded his sister, Bethany, as the two sat down for breakfast.

"Shut up!" growled Ross. "I'll make it when I want to."

Instead of saying the usual table prayer, their dad bowed his head and prayed, "Please forgive us when we aren't kind and friendly. Make us kind to one another as You are to us. In Jesus' name. Amen."

"I wasn't very kind to Ross, but he wasn't very kind to me, either," Bethany said.

"I don't have to be scolded by my sister," said Ross. "She's not my boss."

"No, she isn't your boss, and she shouldn't talk like one," said Mom. "But I don't hear her talk that way very often."

"And I haven't heard anyone say 'shut up' for a long time in this house," said Dad. "I hope I never have to hear it again. It isn't very kind."

"It's pretty hard to be kind all the time when you have a brother," said Bethany, but she was smiling now. Her words were friendly.

"And having some old sister doesn't help either," grumbled Ross, who wasn't quite ready to be kind just yet.

"Ross!" gasped Mom. But now Ross smiled, and they all laughed. They were good friends again. Ross didn't tell Bethany to "shut up" again. He remembered that God had said, "Be kind to one another." He felt better, too. It was fun being kind.

⌒

Let's talk: Was it wrong for Bethany to tell Ross to make his bed? Why were Bethany's words unkind? What was unkind about Ross' answer? What could Bethany have said instead? What could Ross have said? What unkind words are sometimes said in your house? Who is happier—the kind person or the unkind person?

Older children and adults may read: Ephesians 4:32

Let's pray: Please forgive us, dear heavenly Father, for the many unkind words we say. Make us more friendly and kind to people, especially to those in our own home, for Jesus' sake. Amen.

Do not grieve the Holy Spirit [Don't make Him sad].
Ephesians 4:30

Grieving the Holy Spirit

"Mom, when I sin, am I still a child of God?" asked Cara. She was very worried.

"What makes you ask?" her mom questioned.

"Because I made up my mind never to be angry again, but when Drew splashed mud on my new dress, I got real angry at him," Cara said. "I can't always do only what's right."

"You have the same trouble I have," said Mom. "I want to obey God all the time, but I find that I don't always do what's right. Then I ask for forgiveness and try again."

"But are you God's child even when you sin?" asked Cara.

"God always forgives us when we sin," said Mom. "Our sins are always forgiven because Jesus, our Savior, paid for our sins. When you became angry with Drew, you were still God's child. You always are because you have Jesus as your Savior. But your sin grieved the Holy Spirit. It made Him sad."

"What do you mean, Mom?" Cara asked, a little puzzled.

Mom put her arm around Cara. "God the Holy Spirit lives in the hearts of God's children. He lives in your heart," Mom explained. "When you sin, He doesn't move out right away. But you do make Him sad when you sin. The apostle Paul tells us, 'Do not grieve the Holy Spirit.' That means don't make Him sad by sinning. Of course, if you keep on making Him sad, and you don't want Him to stay, then He may leave."

"I want the Holy Spirit to stay in my heart," said Cara.

Let's talk: What was Cara worried about? Did her mother always do God's will? Why was Cara still God's child? Why is God always willing to forgive sins? Where does the Holy Spirit want to live? Why do our sins grieve the Holy Spirit or make Him sad? Why should we not want to grieve the Holy Spirit?

Older children and adults may read: Ephesians 4:25–30

Let's pray: Dear God, please forgive us when we sin. We love Jesus, our Savior. We want to be Your children. Please keep us from making the Holy Spirit sad. In Jesus' name we pray. Amen.

The Lord is good. ... He cares for those who trust in Him.
Nahum 1:7

God Never Forgets His Children

Timothy and Jenna lived on a farm in North Dakota. One winter day they went home from school in a snowstorm. They couldn't see where they were going, and they got lost. They began to cry for help, but nobody could hear them.

"Nobody knows where we are. Nobody can help us," cried Jenna.

"Jenna, somebody *does* know where we are," said Timothy. "God knows."

"Let's pray for help," said Jenna. "Dear Lord Jesus, help us. Please help us."

Soon the two children heard their dog barking nearby. They called to Skipper, and he leaped into Timothy's arms. After some very wet kisses, Skipper led the children back to their house. When they were safe, Timothy and Jenna told their dad that God had sent Skipper.

In the days when the prophet Nahum lived, God's people were often afraid of their enemies. But Nahum told them not to be afraid. He told them to ask God to help them and to depend on Him. He said the Lord cares for those who trust in Him.

What are people afraid of today? Some are afraid of criminals, some are afraid of not having a job, some are sick and afraid they won't get well. God's words in the Bible remind us that He hasn't forgotten us. We know that God won't forget us. We are His children and trust in Him. "The Lord is good. ... He cares for those who trust in Him." He will hear our prayers and answer them.

Let's talk: Why were God's people afraid in the days of Nahum? What did God tell them? What are people afraid of today? What does God tell us? What does "trust in the Lord" mean? Why can we always trust that the Lord will help us? Memorize the Bible verse.

Older children and adults may read: Psalm 91:1–2, 14–16

Let's pray: Dear Lord Jesus, we know that You are good and that You love us. We're sorry that we sometimes become afraid even though we know that we can trust You to always help us. Please forgive us. Send Your Holy Spirit to strengthen our faith in You. In Your name. Amen.

He will command His angels ... to guard you in all your ways. Psalm 91:11

Angel Helpers

Long ago, when the prophet Elisha lived, the king of Syria found out that Elisha was telling his secrets to the king of Israel. Elisha knew the secrets because God told them to him. The king of Syria sent a large army to get Elisha. They came during the night and surrounded the city where Elisha was staying.

The next morning, when Elisha's helper got up, he saw the army surrounding the city. He was very afraid. He went and got Elisha and said, "Look! There are enemy soldiers all around the city. They've come for you. What should we do?"

"Don't worry," Elisha said. "There are more soldiers on our side."

Then Elisha asked God to allow his helper to see the army of angels in the hills. God opened the helper's eyes.

He saw that the enemy army was surrounded by horses and chariots of fire.

Angels are spirits. That's why we can't see them. But they help all God's children, and God sends them to help us, too. What do they do? On some days they may keep things from falling on us and hurting us. On other days they may keep us from walking in front of a car or a bus.

We don't know everything that angels do because we can't see them. But the Bible says, "He will command His angels … to guard you in all your ways." That means they watch over God's children. Aren't you glad?

Let's talk: Why was Elisha's helper afraid? What did God allow him to see? Have you ever seen an angel? Who else in the Bible saw an angel? Memorize the Bible verse.

Older children and adults may read: 2 Kings 6:8–17

Let's pray: Dear God, our Father in heaven, You give us so many good things that we can't see. We thank You for them. We especially thank You for the good angels who help and guard us. Send them to watch over us every day, for Jesus' sake. Amen.

Be thankful. Colossians 3:15

God Wants Us to Be Thankful

Some children whine and cry when they can't have their way. Because they're not thankful for good food to eat, they're so skinny and weak that they just barely squeak. When it's time for a good sleep, they stall and bawl. Something is wrong with them.

God wants His children to be happy. That's why He tells us to be thankful. When we're thankful, we're happy. People who aren't thankful aren't happy.

Asha was never satisfied with anything. She didn't like the clothes her parents gave her to wear. She didn't like the food her parents cooked for her. She didn't ever want to do what she was asked to do. Was she happy? No. She was a very unhappy girl.

The Bible says to be thankful. Just think—God loves us. He forgives all our sins for Jesus' sake. We are His children, and someday Jesus will take us to heaven. That's why we can be thankful in everything. And when we are thankful, Jesus is glad and we're happy.

Let's talk: Why was Asha a very unhappy girl? What does our Bible verse teach us? Why does God want us to be thankful? What are some reasons why we can always be thankful?

Older children and adults may read: Colossians 3:15–17

Let's pray: Dear Father in heaven, we're glad that You always love us and that Jesus died for us on the cross. Help us always to be thankful, especially because we will someday be in heaven with You. In Jesus' name. Amen.

Bless those who curse you. Luke 6:28

How to Treat Mean People

"You're ugly and stupid," Illita said to Lissa.

"Perhaps, I am," said Lissa, "but you're very nice in many ways."

Illita was surprised. Then she looked up and smiled. "You really aren't ugly and stupid," Illita said. Then the girls were friends again.

Suppose Lissa had become angry and said mean words back to Illita. Do you think they would have gotten into a big argument?

Lissa wasn't stupid or dumb. She knew how to avoid an argument and stay friendly. She was bright and sweet.

Jesus told us to do what Lissa did. When somebody says mean things to us, we should say kind things back to them. "Bless those who curse you," Jesus said.

God's children are to treat others kindly even when those people aren't nice to us. They want to do this because it's how God acts. When people say they don't like God or they don't believe in God, God doesn't take their food or shelter away. God is kind and good even to those who don't love Him. His Son, Jesus, died on the cross so that *everyone* could have forgiveness.

If God can be kind to those who are mean to Him, why should we refuse to be kind to those who are mean to us? Jesus wants us to bless those who curse us. God's children should be nice even to those who say hateful things.

⌒

Let's talk: What did Illita say? What did Lissa say? Who said the nicest words? How could Lissa have gotten even? How does God treat people who don't love Him? What does

61

Jesus want us to do when people hate us and curse us? Memorize the Bible verse.

Older children and adults may read: Luke 6:27–31

Let's pray: Dear God, You are good and kind even to those who don't like You. Help us treat others with kindness. Help us say nice things even to those who say mean things to us. We ask this in Jesus' name. Amen.

I have sinned. Luke 15:18

The Hardest Words to Say

Only five children came to school in the big snow-storm. They were trying to solve riddles as they waited for their parents to pick them up.

"Abracadabra is a hard word. Can you say it?" asked Pablo. The other four children tried, but they didn't say it right. They didn't say *it*.

"I know the hardest words for anybody to say," said Justin. "I learned them in Sunday school."

"What words?" the others wanted to know.

"The toughest words to say are 'I have sinned,' " Justin answered.

Do you know what Justin meant? Is it really hard to say, "I have sinned"? Suppose you have a fight and some-one asks, "Who started it?" Does everybody say, "I did"? Or do you all say somebody else sinned?

Suppose you and your friends played with matches and started a fire. Would everybody say, "I did it," or what would you all say?

Jesus told a story about a man's son who left home. He took a lot of money with him and thought he was smart enough to live on his own. It took a long time, and he had a lot of problems before he said, "I have sinned."

But it's good for us to say, "I have sinned." When we say these words to God, He forgives us for Jesus' sake.

Let's talk: Which hard words did Justin learn at Sunday school? Why are those words hard to say? Why is it good for us to say those words to God? For whose sake will our heavenly Father forgive us? How did Jesus pay for our sins?

Older children and adults may read: Luke 15:13–18

Let's pray: Dear heavenly Father, we sin often, and we don't always act like Your children. Please forgive all our sins for Jesus' sake. Help us to be better tomorrow. In His name. Amen.

Turn from evil and do good. Psalm 34:14

Avoiding Sin

"Mom," said Demario, "I wish those bees would leave me alone." Because Demario was standing too close to their nest, the bumblebees were flying close to him.

"Why not move away from the bees," suggested Mom. Demario moved farther from the bushes, and the bees quit bothering him.

Some people say, "I wish my sins would leave me. I want to be good, but I still sin." God's answer is, "Turn away from evil."

Michael and Paige were looking at the berries in their neighbor's garden. They knew it was wrong to pick the berries, but they stood there and looked at them. The more Paige and Michael looked, the more they wanted those berries. Before long they were picking some to eat. They were stealing because they were taking something that didn't belong to them.

What could Michael and Paige have done? They could have walked away or gone inside and finished their chores, or they could have played with their friends. They could have avoided the temptation by moving away from the berries.

Because of Jesus' great love, we want to avoid sin. Sometimes walking away helps. But the best way to avoid sin is to ask Jesus to help you do what is right.

Let's talk: Why were the bees flying around Demario? What was the only way to make them stop? What could Michael and Paige have done to avoid stealing berries? What does the Bible verse say we should do? Who will help us do what is right?

Older children and adults may read: Psalm 34:11–16

Let's pray: Dear Jesus, please help us avoid sin. We know that You had to die on a cross for our sins. Thank you for forgiving us when we don't avoid sin. Help us be the kind of children You want us to be. In Your name. Amen.

The grass withers and the flowers fall, but the Word of our God stands forever. Isaiah 40:8

What the Flowers Said

Chelsea found the prettiest flowers down by the creek and picked a handful for her mother. When she came home, her mother smiled and put them in a vase. The flowers looked very pretty, but a few of them already were drooping.

The next day when Chelsea looked at the flowers, they weren't pretty anymore. They hung over the edges of the vase. Even the grass that was in with the flowers was dried up.

"Mom, your flowers don't look pretty anymore," Chelsea said.

"No, they don't, but they teach us a good lesson," replied Mom.

"What kind of lesson?" asked Chelsea.

Mom put her arm around Chelsea. "The flowers tell us that everything on this earth must die and go away," she explained. "The pretty flowers and the grass die. And do you remember when the big dog the neighbors had died? Even people have to die, like our friend Mr. Peters. Everything that lives on this earth must die."

"Is that what the flowers say, Mom?" Chelsea asked.

"Yes, but they remind us of another thing," Mom added. "They say, 'Only the Word of God will never die.' Everything that God has said will always be true. It stays the same.

"There's a verse in the Bible that says the same thing," Mom continued. "The prophet Isaiah writes, 'The grass withers and the flowers fall, but the Word of our God stands forever.' "

"I'm glad," said Chelsea. "Whoever believes in Jesus will never die. That's what God has promised."

Let's talk: To whom did Chelsea give some flowers? How did they look at first? How did they look the next day? What always happens to flowers and grass? What will always stay the same? Why was Chelsea glad that God's promises will never die?

Older children and adults may read: Isaiah 40:3–8

Let's pray: Dear Father in heaven, we enjoy the pretty flowers that You give us, but we know that they never last long. Help us remember that Your Word will last forever. Make us glad to hear and learn it. Help us share it with others so that we can live together with Jesus forever in heaven. We ask this in His name. Amen.

Jesus Christ is the same yesterday and today and forever.
Hebrews 13:8

Jesus Never Changes

Dana was ready to cry. "Yesterday Kendra was so nice to me, and today she acted so mean," she said with tears in her eyes.

"Some people are like that," said her mom. "But are you sure *you* didn't change? Maybe you were friendly to her yesterday and not very kind today."

"I only told her I didn't like what she said to me," answered Dana.

"Well, most of us change a little every day," Mom explained. "On some days we feel real kind, and on some days we're grouchy. It's a good thing God doesn't change like that, isn't it?"

The Bible says, "Jesus is the same yesterday and today and forever." He never changes. He has always loved everybody in the whole world. He still does. And He always will. We can be sure that Jesus loves us every day and never feels mean or unfriendly to us.

If Jesus' feelings toward us changed every day like ours do, it wouldn't be good for us. We would worry that Jesus might not like us anymore. But Jesus is always the same. He always loves us and forgives us, even when our feelings change and we don't treat others well.

Let's talk: What made Dana feel like crying? What did Mom tell her? Who never changes? Why can we be sure that Jesus loves us all day long, every day? How does Jesus want us to be all the time? Memorize the Bible verse.

Older children and adults may read: John 8:46–58

Let's pray: Dear Jesus, we're glad that You are always the same loving Savior who is always kind and forgiving and helpful. Please make us more like You every day. In Your name we pray. Amen.

If anyone says, "I love God," yet hates his brother, he is a liar. 1 John 4:20

Are You a Liar?

"Look, Mom," said Alex as he showed his mom a card from the Sunday school teacher. It said that Alex was the best student in the class.

"I love God," said Alex. Then he ran out to play next door with Midori.

"Midori," Alex said, "let's go play inside. Here comes that new girl. I don't like her."

Midori and Alex went inside Midori's house to play. The new girl saw the two children go inside. She knew why they had left the yard. She knew they didn't want to be her friends.

The new girl's eyes filled with tears. It hurt to know that people didn't like her just because she was new.

If Jesus wrote report cards, what do you think He might write on one for Alex? He might write, "Alex is a liar." God tells us in our Bible verse, "If anyone says, 'I love God,' yet hates his brother, he is a liar." Alex knew how much God loved him. Alex said that he loved God, but he wasn't nice to the new girl.

Perhaps Alex didn't know that he was hurting somebody. Midori's mother looked out the window and said, "You know, that little girl who just moved in down the street probably doesn't have any friends to play with. I'm going to give her some of my cookies."

When Alex saw what Midori's mother was doing, he remembered how God loves all people. "May we take the cookies to her?" Alex asked. And the children played together the rest of the day.

⁓

Let's talk: How did Alex show that he loved God? How did Alex treat the new girl? Who showed Alex a better way? What does God call people who say they love Him but do not love those around them? What did Jesus do for all people? Is there anyone whom Jesus does not love? Memorize the Bible verse.

Older children and adults may read: 1 John 4:19–21

Let's pray: Dear Jesus, help us to love others as You loved us and all people. Amen.

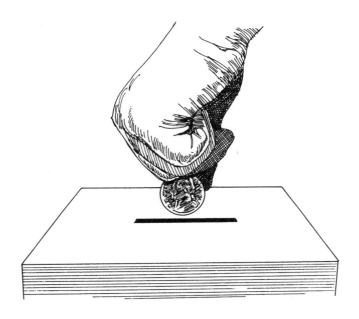

Do everything without complaining. Philippians 2:14

The Grumble Box

Over at the Stockton home the children were always complaining. When the food was hot, they complained. When the food was cold, they complained. They complained when they were called to eat, and they complained when dinner was late. Even Mr. Stockton complained.

One day Mrs. Stockton said, "You know, we shouldn't complain all the time. God says, 'Do everything without complaining.'

"God wants us to be cheerful people, willing to do whatever is good," Mrs. Stockton continued. "I put a slot in the top of this box. Every time we complain, we're going to put five cents in the box. Maybe that will help us learn not to complain."

The whole family agreed to give it a try. They put the box in the middle of the table. Whoever complained had to put five cents in the box. Eventually, the Stocktons learned to smile and not to complain. At the end of the first month, Dad counted the money in the box. There was $10.65. The youngest Stockton took it to Sunday school and put it in the offering basket.

Some people complain no matter where they are. They complain at church. They complain at work. They complain when it's hot. They complain when it rains. They just complain too much.

But don't we complain, too? We complain when we have to do something we don't like to do. We aren't always cheerful. Maybe we forget that we're God's children and that we aren't showing thankfulness to God when we complain.

When the apostle Paul wrote the Bible verse about complaining, he was talking about how we should act when we do what Jesus wants us to do. But what he said is true at all times: "Do everything without complaining."

Let's talk: What did the children complain about in the Stockton home? How did Mrs. Stockton try to stop them? Why do some people complain wherever they are? What do we complain about in our house? What does the Bible verse tell us?

Older children and adults may read: Luke 15:25–32

Let's pray: Dear Lord Jesus, please make us satisfied, cheerful, and thankful. We have so many reasons to be happy. Keep us from complaining. Because we know that You love us, make us willing and glad to do what You want. In Your name. Amen.

Let us love one another. 1 John 4:7

Do You Love All People?

Mr. Affton went to church every Sunday. He knew his Bible well. He was nice to people, and people were nice to him.

But there was one man Mr. Affton wasn't nice to—Mr. Ballwin. The problem began in a meeting when the two men had a disagreement. Mr. Ballwin called Mr. Affton a fool. Mr. Affton never forgot that comment, and he never forgave Mr. Ballwin for saying it.

At church Mr. Affton didn't sit anywhere near Mr. Ballwin. He wouldn't talk to him or look at him. Mr. Affton hated Mr. Ballwin. When you don't like someone day after day, you hate that person.

One day in church Mr. Affton heard a sermon about love. "Dear friends, let us love one another," the pastor read from the Bible. Then the pastor described how God loved all people so much that He sent His only Son, Jesus, to die for us and to pay for our sins.

Mr. Affton began to think about what the pastor was saying. "God is love," he heard the pastor say. "Because God so loved us, we also should love one another."

Right then and there Mr. Affton knew that he couldn't love God if he hated Mr. Ballwin. He asked Jesus to forgive him, and from then on, he was friendly to Mr. Ballwin.

Let's talk: How do you feel when you hate someone? How did God show that He loves everyone? With Jesus' love inside us, will we love others or hate them? If we keep on hating a person, will Jesus stay in our heart? Memorize the Bible verse.

Older children and adults may read: 1 John 4:19–21

Let's pray: Dear loving Father in heaven, You are so willing to forgive us and to love us even though we have sinned. Please make us willing to love others for Jesus' sake. In His name. Amen.

[Jesus said,] "Come to Me ... and I will give you rest."
Matthew 11:28

Where to Find Rest

Megan's rabbit got out of its cage, and a dog chased it. The rabbit hopped here and there, trying to find a safe place to rest, but the dog kept chasing it. The rabbit was almost too tired to hop anymore. Then Megan came outside, and the rabbit hopped up to her. She picked the rabbit up and put it in her lap. The dog ran away. Now the rabbit could rest.

Sometimes people are just like that rabbit. They are chased by troubles or worries. One boy didn't have any friends, and he worried about it. A girl wasn't getting good grades in school, and she was upset about it. Another girl was often sick, and it made her sad. Sometimes our troubles chase us like a dog chases a rabbit.

The world is full of troubles, and the worst trouble is sin. A mother told her daughter not to open the cabinet with the good dishes, but she did anyway. That was a sin. When she broke a dish, she lied and said she didn't do it. That was another sin. That night she couldn't sleep because she knew she had sinned. Sin brings trouble.

To everyone with troubles, Jesus says, "Come to Me … and I will give you rest." Like the scared rabbit that hopped to Megan, we can go to Jesus. We go to Him when we pray or when we just think about Him and His love for us.

The little girl prayed to Jesus to take away her sin. Then she went downstairs and told her mother she was sorry she had lied about the dish. After that she went back to bed and fell asleep. Jesus gave her rest.

Let's talk: Where did Megan's rabbit find rest? Where does Jesus say we can find rest? What troubles do people have? What troubles do we have in our family? What will Jesus do for us? Memorize the Bible verse.

Older children and adults may read: John 14:1–3

Let's pray: Thank You for Your promise, dear Jesus, that You will give us rest when we come to You. We know that You forgive all our sins because You love us. That's why we love You. In Your name. Amen.

Blessed are the peacemakers. Matthew 5:9

The Peacemakers

"Come on, we don't want any fights. Let's be friends and play ball," Akeem told Jerome and Philip. Akeem was a peacemaker because Jerome and Philip quit arguing.

"Mrs. Oliver didn't say any bad things about you," said Mrs. Simon to her neighbor. "She said you were kind."

"Oh, did she?" said the neighbor. "Well, I guess she's a friend after all." Mrs. Simon was a peacemaker.

When the Civil War was over, many people in the North hated the people in the South. Abraham Lincoln didn't. He wanted them all to be friends. Abraham Lincoln was a peacemaker.

All people on earth were disobeying God. God had to punish them. Jesus said, "Let Me take their punishment." So He was punished for us. Now we have peace with God. Jesus is our great Peacemaker.

"Believe in Jesus as your Savior," said the missionary to the head of an African village. "Ask Him to take away your sins. He will do it." The African man believed that Jesus was his Savior. He believed that Jesus had paid for his sins. Now he had peace with God. The missionary was a peacemaker.

The Bible says, "Blessed are the peacemakers."

Let's talk: How did Akeem make peace? How did Mrs. Simon make peace between her neighbors? Why is Abraham Lincoln called a peacemaker? How did Jesus make peace for us with God? How can we be peacemakers?

Older children and adults may read: Matthew 5:1–9

Let's pray: Dear heavenly Father, so many people hate and fight. Help us make peace wherever we can, especially by telling people about the peace they can have with You through Jesus, their Savior. In His name we ask this. Amen.

Speak evil of no one. Titus 3:2 (RSV)

Telling the Truth Can Be Wrong

Mr. Coleman was a mean man. He always said what he thought and told what he knew, even if it hurt other people. He felt that if he thought it, he might as well say it. "I say what I think. And if it's true, why shouldn't I?" Mr. Coleman often said. Was he right?

No, he was very wrong. A new family moved to Mr. Coleman's town. The man had been in jail, but he was sorry for what he had done. He tried to get a job, but Mr. Coleman told people that he had been in jail. Nobody wanted to hire the man because of what Mr. Coleman said.

It isn't only wrong to tell lies, it's also wrong when you tell the truth and it hurts someone. God says, "Speak evil of no one." It's always wrong to say something bad about a person, even when it's true, if you are only trying to hurt that person. Of course, sometimes you do need to tell an adult if someone is doing something that can hurt you or someone else. Ask Jesus to help you know what to say.

◦

Let's talk: What kind of man was Mr. Coleman? Did Mr. Coleman tell a lie about the new man in town? Why was it wrong for him to tell the truth? When is it wrong to tell the truth? What does the Bible verse say?

Older children and adults may read: 1 Peter 2:21–24

Let's pray: Lord Jesus, we wish we could always be kind and helpful like You. Please forgive us when we say things that hurt other people. Help us tell only what is kind and helpful. Please make us more like You. In Your name. Amen.

Christ … [left] you an example, that you should follow in His steps. 1 Peter 2:21

Following Jesus

It had been snowing. Mrs. Sutherland was walking to the store. On the way she heard a voice behind her.

"Mommy, I'm stepping in your steps," called her daughter, Kali. She was following, trying to step right where Mommy's steps were in the snow.

When Mrs. Sutherland noticed what Kali was trying to do, she took smaller steps. When Kali became tired, she carried her the rest of the way.

Children like to do what their parents do. Because we believe in Jesus, we're God's children. We want to do what Jesus did. The Bible tells us that Jesus left us an example that we should follow in His steps.

But aren't Jesus' steps too big for us to follow? Yes, they are, if He doesn't help us. But He became a baby and grew up like any other boy. He lived on earth for us and made His steps small so that we could follow them. And He died on the cross to pay for the wrong steps we take.

When do you follow the steps of Jesus? You follow Jesus when your mom or dad ask you to help with the dishes, and you think, "Jesus would do it," and then you help. You follow Jesus when you see your friend's baseball glove lying out in the rain and you pick it up because that's what Jesus would do. Whenever we try to do what Jesus would do, we are following in His footsteps.

Remember, Christ left us an example, that we should follow in His steps.

Let's talk: How can we follow in Jesus' steps? Do we follow Jesus when we do wrong? What are some things Jesus did when He was on earth? What are some things we can do to follow Jesus? Memorize the Bible verse.

Older children and adults may read: John 12:26

Let's pray: Thank You for Your good example, dear Lord Jesus. Help us all do what You would do. Please forgive us when we don't. In Your name. Amen.

Do not ... bear a grudge. Leviticus 19:18

Don't Bear a Grudge

"What's a grudge?" asked Mr. Cardwell, the third-grade teacher.

"I know," said Joshua. "It's a place where you keep your car." He was thinking of a garage.

But that wasn't what Mr. Cardwell meant. What he meant was when somebody hurts you and you never smile at that person again. When you "bear a grudge," you can't forget a mean thing somebody did to you. God says, "Do not bear a grudge."

Caitlyn came home from playing with her friends. "Mom, I will never talk to Lana again. She said I was dirty," Caitlyn said with a determined look on her face.

For several days, Caitlyn bore a grudge against Lana. She kept those hurt feelings inside and wouldn't even speak to Lana.

But bearing a grudge is wrong. It's like hating somebody. God doesn't want us to hate. He wants us to love. What would happen if God hated us when we sinned? What if God wouldn't forgive us? Then we would never get to heaven.

But God loves us even though we sin. He sent Jesus to die for us. Because God loved us that much, we want to find ways to love others, too, even if they aren't always as nice as we want them to be.

∾

Let's talk: What did Joshua think a grudge was? What is a grudge? When do people bear grudges? Why is it wrong to bear a grudge? Why does God forgive us everything we have done wrong? Why are we willing to forgive others? Memorize the Bible verse.

Older children and adults may read: Leviticus 19:16–18

Let's pray: Dear Lord, You love us enough to forgive our sins every day. Please make us loving, too, so that we will forgive other people as you forgive us. Amen.

I have strayed like a lost sheep. Psalm 119:176

When Sheep Get Lost

Mr. Keck was a rancher. He had many sheep. When they were eating grass, they behaved very well. But if one of them walked away from the place they were eating, they all wanted to walk away.

Once one of the sheep saw a hole in the fence and went through. So did the next sheep, and the next one, until all the sheep had gone through the hole.

Fluffy, a particularly frisky lamb, went through the hole too. When the neighbor's dog started barking, the sheep became afraid. They tried to find the hole in the fence, but they forgot where it was. They ran all over the field. One sheep broke a leg. One got caught in some bushes and couldn't get loose. Fluffy jumped over some tall grass and landed in a mud puddle. He was a very scared little lamb by the time Mr. Keck found him.

God says that we wander off just like sheep. Sheep don't have much sense about what's right, and we don't either. We do so many things we shouldn't. We fight. We tell lies. We don't obey our parents. And we don't do the things God wants us to do. All this is sin.

What can we do about sin? We can tell God about it and ask Him to forgive us and take us back. We tell God about our sins when we say with the Bible verse, "I have strayed like a lost sheep."

Let's talk: Why does God say that we are like sheep? When do people stray like sheep? What are some things we often do wrong? Who is the Good Shepherd who saves us from our sins?

Older children and adults may read: Psalm 119:174–176

Let's pray: Dear God, our Father in heaven, we often are as foolish as sheep. We stray away and do things You don't want us to do. Please forgive us and bring us back again to where we are safe with You. We ask this in Jesus' name. Amen.

The highway of the upright avoids evil. Proverbs 16:17

The Right Highway

The first time Mr. Devon tried to drive to Highland, he came to an intersection. One highway turned right; the other went straight. Which one should he take? He didn't know.

He looked at the signs at the intersection. One sign said: "Highland—2 miles," and it pointed to the right. Then he knew which highway to take.

Our whole life is like a highway. Sometimes we don't know which turn to take.

Tara went to a store. She wished she could buy some candy, but she didn't have any money. The check-out person was in the back helping someone. Tara could have taken some candy. We could call that way the "Stealing Street." But Tara didn't turn down that road. She didn't take the candy; she stayed on the "Honest Highway."

Enrique was asked to go to a picnic, but his mother got sick and needed his help at home. His mother told him to go to the picnic. "But Jesus would want me to help you, Momma," said Enrique. Enrique stayed home. He didn't take "Me-First Highway." He turned onto the "Street of Love."

In the Bible, God tells us which highway to take. He wants us to take the highway of the upright. The upright are those who trust in the Lord and do what is right. And the highway of the upright avoids evil. To live correctly, we also must turn away from whatever is wrong.

Let's talk: How did Mr. Devon know which highway to take? In what book can we read God's signs? Which highway did Tara choose when she was tempted to take some candy? Which highway did Enrique take when he stayed at home to help his mother? Can you think of someone else who took the right highway? What are some highways we will want to take to do what is right? Memorize the Bible verse.

Older children and adults may read: Proverbs 16:16–20

Let's pray: Dear God, help us understand Your directions in the Bible. Give us a willing spirit to follow them so we will avoid evil. When we make a wrong turn, bring us back to the right highway for Jesus' sake. In His name. Amen.

If a man will not work, he shall not eat. 2 Thessalonians 3:10

The Right to Eat

A professor had a pile of stones in one corner of his yard. A homeless person came to his door one day and asked, "Would you please give a hungry man something to eat?"

"I'll be glad to," answered the professor. "If you'll move that pile of stones into the other corner of my yard, I'll give you a meal for your work."

The homeless person didn't want to work. So the professor didn't give him anything to eat.

The professor kept the stones to test people's willingness to work. Every time a needy person came to his house, the professor asked the person to move the stones in exchange for a meal. Those who worked, ate; those who wouldn't work didn't eat.

Maybe there are better ways to test a person's willingness to work, but the professor was trying to live by the Word of God: "If a man will not work, he shall not eat."

Every child of God wants to be useful. We won't be useful if we don't learn to work. When children are small, they can't do much. Children have a lot of time to play, but they can begin to do little things. They can pick up their toys and help around the house. As they grow older, they are able to do more. If they learn how to work, someday they may have an important job.

God wants us to learn to be good workers. If someone is too sick to work or there is no work for them to do, we should be glad to help them. But if anyone is not willing to work, they don't have the right to eat.

≈

Let's talk: Why did the professor ask needy people to move the pile of stones? Can people be useful and helpful if they don't want to work? Why does God want His children to learn to work? What great work did Jesus do to make us God's children?

Older children and adults may read: 2 Thessalonians 3:7–12

Let's pray: Dear Father in heaven, we're glad that You want us to be workers because we want to do things for You. Please make us good workers who are glad to be useful and helpful. Thank You for sending Your Son to work for us. We pray this in Jesus' name. Amen.

Out of the heart come evil thoughts. Matthew 15:19

Where Sins Come From

Donzell had a dream. He dreamed that all his sisters and brothers, his father and mother, and all the neighbors could see everything he was thinking. Even when he thought something that was bad, everybody could see it. In his dream, he ran away because he didn't think anybody would love him anymore.

Donzell was glad when he woke up and realized it was only a dream. It was bad enough to think bad things, but to have people see them would be terrible. He was glad that no one could really see what he was thinking.

Would you like it if people could always see what you were thinking? All of us think bad things sometimes. All the bad things we do come from our thinking. Why do we say mean words? Because we first think and feel them. Why do we do mean things? Because we think of doing them.

Jesus said, "Out of the heart come evil thoughts." And when we think wrong, we do wrong. Jesus forgives our wrong thoughts and deeds and wants us to think only good things. He will help us do it.

⁓

Let's talk: Why did Donzell want to run away? Why would you not want everyone to see what you're thinking? How many people are there who never think bad things? Where does our wrong thinking come from? Who washes away our sins and cleans our heart?

Older children and adults may read: Matthew 15:18–20

Let's pray: Dear Father in heaven, please take away all the bad and mean things we think and do. Make our hearts clean and our thinking right by giving us Your Holy Spirit. We ask this for Jesus' sake, who died to save us. Amen.

[It is] better to be poor than a liar. Proverbs 19:22

A Poor Rich Man

Naaman, a general who had fought against God's people, went to the prophet Elisha to be healed from a disease called leprosy. Elisha told Naaman to wash in the Jordan River seven times. When Naaman believed and obeyed, God healed him. Naaman returned to Elisha and wanted to give him some gifts. But Elisha didn't want Naaman to think that God expected something in return for healing him, so he refused the gifts.

Later, Gehazi, Elisha's helper, ran after Naaman. He told the general that Elisha had changed his mind and wanted some money and some clothes for some new students. Naaman gave Gehazi some money and two sets of clothing. Gehazi hid these in his house.

But Elisha knew what his helper had done. When Gehazi returned to Elisha, the prophet asked him, "Where were you, Gehazi?"

Gehazi lied and said he hadn't been anywhere. But Elisha knew he had lied and told him, "From now on you will have Naaman's sickness." Suddenly Gehazi's skin became as white as snow from leprosy. It didn't pay for Gehazi to lie.

Do we get sick when we tell lies? No. God doesn't send sickness to punish us. God sent Jesus to take the punishment for our lies and for all our other sins. Because Jesus loves us so much, we want to say only what is true.

It would have been better if Gehazi had stayed poor and honest instead of becoming rich and a liar. That's what God says in our Bible verse, "It is better to be poor than a liar."

Let's talk: What is so bad about telling lies? Why did Gehazi tell Naaman a lie? How was Gehazi punished by God? How many people in the world have never told a lie? For whose sake is God eager to forgive us? Why will we want to keep from lying?

Older children and adults may read: 2 Kings 5:20–27

Let's pray: Dear Father in heaven, we're glad that everything You have said is true, especially Your promises of forgiveness and love. Help us say only what is true. We pray this in Jesus' name. Amen.

I will sing to the Lord all my life. Psalm 104:33

Singing to the Lord

Karissa was feeling sad. So what did she do? She started to sing. "Count your blessings, name them one by one, and it will surprise you what the Lord has done," she sang.

Then Karissa counted what the Lord had done for her. "I have a good home while many people lost theirs in the flood," she said. "I have good clothes—well, anyway, clothes; a cute baby brother; and so many other things. Best of all, I have Jesus as my Friend and Savior, and I know that God loves me.

"Count your blessings, name them one by one," she continued singing. Soon she wasn't sad anymore.

Did you ever sing to the Lord when you didn't feel good? It helps you feel thankful and happy.

Do you ever feel that nobody loves you? Sing "Jesus Loves Me." It will remind you that you always have a best Friend who loves you no matter what. Try singing "What a Friend We Have in Jesus" to remind you how special His friendship is. When you're worried about something, sing "I Am Trusting You, Lord Jesus." It will remind you that Jesus is always ready to help you.

While you wait for Sunday school or church to begin, memorize verses to your favorite songs. Then when you need them, you'll have them in your mind so you can sing them.

People who know and love God say, "I will sing to the Lord all my life." They're happy when they think of how much God loves them.

Let's talk: What did Karissa do when she felt sad? Why does singing help us feel better? What other hymns do you know? Why do we want to sing to the Lord as long as we live? Memorize the Bible verse.

Older children and adults may read: Psalm 105:1–5

Let's pray: Thank You, dear Lord, for Your wonderful love that comforts us when we are sad and puts a song in our hearts. When we sing our thanks and our joy to You, accept our prayers for Jesus' sake. Amen.

Teach me Your way, O Lord. Psalm 86:11

Learning God's Way

Amy asked her dad to go to Sunday school and church with her.

"No, I'm staying home," her dad said. "You can go if you want to. You go your way, and I'll go mine."

"Dad, which way are you going?" Amy asked.

Dad grunted, but he didn't answer. He thought about Amy's question for a long time.

Which way am I going? he asked himself. I'm going the wrong way. I'm not going God's way, he told himself.

The Holy Spirit was making Amy's dad think. While Amy was at church, Dad tried to read the comics, but he couldn't. At last he prayed, "Dear God, please help me to go Your way."

Because the Holy Spirit had worked faith in the heart of Amy's dad, he was able to ask what our Bible verse asks: "Teach me Your way, O Lord." Amy's dad began to read the Bible and go to church. He learned that God's way to heaven is through believing in Jesus and following Him.

Because we are God's children, we want to go God's way. But how do we know God's way? God teaches us His way in His book, the Bible. The Bible shows us our sins and it shows us our Savior, Jesus. It also teaches us how to live as a Christian.

God teaches us His way when we read the Bible during devotions or at church, or even when we read a Bible story book. He wants us to study the Bible whenever we can. Because we are God's children, we say, "Teach me Your way, O Lord."

Let's talk: What did Amy ask her dad to do? Why didn't Amy's dad want to go to church? What did he tell Amy he was doing? What question did Amy ask that started her father thinking? What happened while Amy was at church? In what book does God tell us His way? How can even a little child learn God's way?

Older children and adults may read: Psalm 86:9–12

Let's pray: Dear God, make us willing to learn Your way and help us to follow it, for Jesus' sake. Amen.

It is more blessed to give than to receive. Acts 20:35

Giving and Receiving

Trent wanted some extra money for a new baseball. He wrote his mom a note and put it on her plate at suppertime. It said:

Mother owes Trent:

For helping around the house	$1.50
For making his bed	$1.00
For picking up his clothes	$1.00
For loading the dishwasher	$2.00
For practicing piano	$2.00
Total	$7.50

At breakfast the next morning Trent found $10 on his plate. There was also a note that said:

Trent owes Mom:

For three good meals a day	Nothing
For washing his clothes	Nothing
For taking care of him when sick	Nothing
For a good home and lots of love	Nothing
For teaching him	Nothing
Total	Nothing

How do you think Trent felt when he read his mother's note? He probably was ashamed of what he had written. The Bible says, "It is more blessed to give than to receive." This means that it's better to give than to get. Giving makes us happier than getting.

Did you ever notice how unhappy people are who always get everything and never learn to give? People who share what they have and try to help others are happy people. Jesus came to give everyone His love and help. He even gave His life to save us all. That's why He is such a wonderful Savior. We show Jesus how thankful we are for His good gifts when we give to others instead of just getting.

Let's talk: How did Trent try to get some extra money? What was his mother giving Trent for nothing? What does the Bible verse say about giving? Which people are happier—those who give or those who receive? What did Jesus give to all people when He died on the cross? Why does giving make us happy?

Older children and adults may read: Acts 20:32–38

Let's pray: Dear heavenly Father, we're glad that You have given us Jesus as our Savior. Help us to be happy by giving instead of only trying to get things. For Jesus' sake we ask this. Amen.

You are My friends if you do what I command. John 15:14

How to Be Friends with Jesus

Dillon came into the house crying. "C. J. isn't my friend," he sobbed.

"Why isn't C. J. your friend?" asked his mom.

"Because she won't do what I tell her," said Dillon. Dillon had wanted C. J. to go to the store with him, but C. J. wouldn't.

Most of the time, C. J. did what Dillon wanted and Dillon did what C. J. wanted, and they were good friends. But when C. J. didn't do what Dillon wanted or when Dillon didn't do what C. J. wanted, they weren't friends. The more they did for each other, the better friends they were.

That's what our friendship with Jesus should be like. Because Jesus loved us so much that He died for us to make us His friends, we want to do the things He asks us to do.

Jesus said, "You are My friends if you do what I command."

What does Jesus want us to do? He wants us to obey His commands in the Bible—obey our parents, help others, be honest, don't hurt others with our words or actions, and believe that He is our Savior from sin.

Just before Jesus said the words in our Bible verse, He also said, "Love each other as I have loved you." That's especially what He meant when He said, "You are My friends if you do what I tell you."

Let's talk: How can you tell when two people are very good friends? How does Jesus want His friends to treat one another? How does the Holy Spirit help us do what Jesus commands us to do? Memorize the Bible verse.

Older children and adults may read: John 15:4–8

Let's pray: Dear Jesus, we want to be Your friends and Your followers. Please forgive us when we don't do what You command us to do. Help us do those things that You want us to do so that everyone will see that we are Your friends. In Your name. Amen.

Your will be done on earth as it is in heaven. Matthew 6:10

Let God Decide

A pastor named Moody once took his daughter Emma to a store to buy her a doll. As soon as they entered the store, Emma picked out the doll that she wanted.

"This is the one I want," Emma exclaimed, holding it tightly in her arms. It wasn't as nice as the one her father wanted to get for her, but because her mind was made up, he bought it for her.

The inexpensive doll was soon left in a corner of Emma's room. One day Emma's father told her that he had wanted to buy her a much bigger and prettier doll than the one she had picked out.

"Why didn't you?" she asked.

"Because you wouldn't let me," he reminded her.

Emma was sorry she had wanted her own way. She decided to let her father decide what to give her. When he asked Emma what he should bring her from a trip, she would say, "Whatever you would like me to have." She learned to trust her father's love for her.

In the prayer Jesus taught us, He told us to say to our Father in heaven, "Your will be done." Our Father in heaven loves us more than Pastor Moody loved Emma. God even sent His Son, Jesus, to die for us so that we could have forgiveness and a home in heaven. God wants us to be His happy children. He knows what is best for us, so we can trust Him to decide what we need.

Let's talk: What mistake did Emma make? Why would her father have given her a pretty doll? What did Emma learn? How did she show what she had learned? Why did Jesus tell us to say "Your will be done" to our Father in heaven?

Right before Jesus died on the cross, He prayed to God in the Garden of Gethsemane. He said, "Not as I will, but as You will." What did He mean? Have we learned to say that?

Older children and adults may read: Luke 22:39–43

Let's pray: Dear Lord Jesus, thank You very much for doing Your Father's will so that we could be saved. Help us say, "Your will be done," and really mean it. We love you. Amen.

As the mountains surround Jerusalem, so the Lord surrounds His people. Psalm 125:2

God Protects His People

Before there were guns and airplanes, people liked to build their cities on mountains or very high hills. These cities were safer from enemies than those built on flat ground.

King David built the city of Jerusalem on a hill that had mountains surrounding it. This city was extra safe because even a few soldiers could stop a big army from coming too close. Soldiers protecting the city could fight in places between the mountains where only a few enemy soldiers could get through at a time.

David thought of how God protects us like the mountains protect Jerusalem. He wrote about how safe God's people are when they trust Him. "As the mountains surround Jerusalem, so the Lord surrounds His people," King David wrote.

But the mountains didn't always save Jerusalem. When the people in Jerusalem became wicked, God allowed enemies to come and burn the city. As long as the people believed and loved God, God protected them.

God can protect us even when mountains can't. Because we belong to Jesus, nothing can hurt us. God always takes care of His people.

⤢

Let's talk: How did mountains protect people long ago? Why did King David think that God was like the mountains? Why couldn't the mountains keep the people of Jerusalem safe when they were wicked? Why are God's children always safe? Memorize the Bible verse.

Older children and adults may read: Psalm 125

Let's pray: Dear heavenly Father, with so many dangers around us, we need You to protect us like a mountain. Keep us in Your loving arms so we will be safe from all harm and danger. In Jesus' name. Amen.

I can do everything through [Jesus] who gives me strength. Philippians 4:13

How Can We Be Strong?

"I can't do it. I just can't do it," exclaimed Matthew as he walked into the house.

"What can't you do?" asked his dad.

"I can't pick up that big stone in the yard. It won't move. It's too heavy," Matthew answered.

"Well, maybe we can move it together," said Dad. "I'll help you." Matthew and his dad went outside, and with his dad's help, Matthew moved the big stone easily.

There are many things we can't do by ourselves. We often say, "I can't do it." But the apostle Paul said, "I can do everything through Jesus who gives me strength."

With Jesus' help, we can do anything. Isn't it good to have Jesus as a Friend and Helper?

Of course, Jesus won't help us with things He doesn't want us to do. But whatever is right and pleasing to God, Jesus will help us do. He makes us strong even though we are very weak. "Everything is possible for him who believes," Jesus said.

Let's talk: Why couldn't Matthew lift the stone by himself? Who helped Matthew do what he couldn't do alone? What are some things we can't do by ourselves? What does the Bible verse say? Why is Jesus able to help us do anything that God wants?

Older children and adults may read: 2 Corinthians 12:7–10

Let's pray: Dear Jesus, our Lord and Savior and Helper, we know that with Your help we can do anything. Help us fight against the devil's temptation. Please help us do whatever our Father in heaven wants us to do. In Your name. Amen.

Underneath are the everlasting arms. Deuteronomy 33:27

What God's Care Is Like

Long ago Moses wrote, "Underneath are the everlasting arms." What do you think he meant?

Was he thinking of a boy jumping from a chair into his mother's arms? God's care is like a mother's arms.

Was he thinking of a girl whose father carried her over some water? God's care is like a father's arms.

Was he thinking of an eagle? The mother eagle flies under her young eagles while they are learning to fly. If they fall, the mother eagle catches them on her back and flies them safely back to the nest.

The everlasting arms under us are God's arms. We can't see God's arms, but God tells us that nothing bad can happen to His children because "underneath are the everlasting arms."

God's arms are everlasting—they never get tired, and they're never too weak to help us, and they're always under us.

Let's talk: Do your parents ever hold you or carry you in their arms? Could your father or mother ever drop you? Why don't God's arms ever get tired and weak? God's arms are always under you. He takes care of you in everything.

Older children and adults may read: Psalm 46:1–3

Let's pray: Dear heavenly Father, we're thankful that Your arms are under and around Your children at all times. Hold us close to You. When we fall into sin or any trouble, reach out and save us, for Jesus' sake. Amen.

Jesus answered, "I am the Way." John 14:6

The Escalator to Heaven

Emily always liked to go with her mother to the big department store. She would stand on the bottom step, and the escalator would take her up to the next floor. "I like to ride the escalator," Emily told her little brother, Jesse.

"What's an escalator?" Jesse asked.

"It has steps that move," Emily explained. "You don't walk up. The steps carry you up."

"Wow!" Jesse exclaimed. "Jesus is like an escalator. He takes people up to heaven."

When Jesus lived on earth, Thomas, one of His disciples, asked, "How can we know the way to where you are going?"

Jesus didn't just say He would show Thomas the way. He said, "I am the Way." Jesus doesn't just show people how to get to heaven, He takes them there Himself. Jesus is kind of like an escalator. Because we believe in Jesus and love Him and trust Him, we're on the way to heaven.

Let's talk: What is an escalator? Why did Jesse call Jesus an escalator? What did Jesus' disciple Thomas ask? What was Jesus' answer? How do we get to heaven?

Older children and adults may read: John 14:1–6

Let's pray: Dear Jesus, we're glad that You are the Way to heaven. We know that we can't get there by ourselves. Please keep us close to You every day so that we will always be on the way to heaven. We ask this because we know that You are our Lord and Savior. Amen.

[God has] filled my heart with greater joy. Psalm 4:7

When You're Happy Inside

"When Mrs. Youngman smiles, I don't think she means it," said Gabriella. "She just smiles a little bit with her mouth and then stops."

"It's hard to smile on the outside when you don't smile on the inside, isn't it?" said her mother.

"Yeah," agreed Gabriella, "so I thought I would bring Mrs. Youngman some flowers. Maybe that will make her smile inside, and then her outside smile will look better."

"That's a good idea," said Mother. "You know, you reminded me of a Bible verse that tells how to get happy on the inside."

"What is it?" asked Gabriella.

"It's something King David said in a psalm. He wrote that God had filled his heart with greater joy," Mother answered.

"What made King David say that, Mom?" asked Gabriella.

Mother looked in her Bible at Psalm 4. "Well, first David said to God, 'Have mercy on me, and hear my prayer.' Then he said to himself, 'The Lord will hear when I call to Him.' So I guess God made him happy by promising to love and help him."

"God loves us, too," said Gabriella.

"You know He does," said Mother. "He even gave His Son, Jesus, to die for us on the cross. Jesus died to pay for our sins, and now God forgives us and smiles at us."

"If God is smiling at us, He really means it, doesn't He?" said Gabriella.

"He certainly does," said Mother. "And when we know that He loves us, it makes us glad inside. Then we can smile on the outside, too."

Let's talk: What bothered Gabriella? Why was it hard for Mrs. Youngman to smile on the outside? What made King David happy in his heart? How do you know that God loves you? How do you feel on the inside because you know God is smiling at you? When you're happy on the inside, how do you show it on the outside?

Older children and adults may read: Psalm 4

Let's pray: You have put gladness in our hearts, dear God. Please help us remember that You love us. Then we will always be happy on the inside, and it will be easy to smile on the outside and really mean it. We ask this in Jesus' name. Amen.

Jesus said, "Father, forgive them, for they do not know what they are doing." Luke 23:34

What We Do When We Sin

Demond was playing ball in his back yard. He stepped on some flowers his mother had just planted. "I didn't know I was doing it," said Demond when his mother called to him. His mother saw that Demond really didn't know he was trampling her flowers, so she forgave him.

When Jesus was ready to die for us, some soldiers took Him and nailed Him to a cross. They had to do it; their officer told them to do it. But they didn't know that it was their Savior they were nailing on the cross. They didn't know that Jesus was their Lord and God.

So Jesus prayed for them as they pounded nails into His hands and feet. "Father, forgive them," He said, "because they do not know what they are doing." Jesus loved even the men who were hurting Him.

When we do wrong, we hurt Jesus more than the nails hurt Him. Jesus had to die for all our sins. But He willingly died because He knew it was part of God's plan to save us.

Jesus also prays for us, just like He prayed for the soldiers. He still says, "Father, forgive them for they do not know what they are doing." As we remember Jesus' prayer and His love for us, our Savior will help us keep from sinning.

Let's talk: What did the soldiers do to Jesus? How did Jesus pray for them? Why did Jesus let the soldiers nail Him to a cross? What does Jesus want His Father to do for us? How does Jesus' love for us help us turn away from sin?

Older children and adults may read: Luke 23:33–43

Let's pray: Dear Jesus, You were so kind when the soldiers were hurting You. Please ask Your Father to forgive our sins, too. Help us remember that our sins also hurt You. Keep us from doing wrong, because we love You. Amen.

God loves a cheerful giver. 2 Corinthians 9:7

Do You Like to Give Things?

"Mom, I don't want to give Lacey anything for her birthday this year," said Miriam. "She never gives me anything."

"You know she can't afford to give you presents," said her mom. "Lacey's parents are very poor. Do you give presents so you can get some back?"

Miriam shrugged her shoulders and hung her head, feeling a little ashamed.

Mom put her arm around Miriam. "You'll never be happy if you give to get," she said. "Do you know what the Bible says about giving?"

"What?" Miriam asked.

"Well, it says we should give what is in our hearts. We shouldn't give what we don't want to or because we have to. The Bible says 'God loves a cheerful giver,' " Mom explained.

"You mean God wants us to be happy when we give things to other people?" asked Miriam.

"Yes," said Mom. "He gave us His Son, Jesus, as a gift. He also gives us His love and anything else we need."

"Jesus wants us to help poor people, doesn't He?" said Miriam.

"Yes, that's one way of showing our love for Jesus," said Mom.

"Can I take a big cake to Lacey for her birthday?" Miriam asked. "She never has a birthday cake."

"God loves a cheerful giver," Mom said as she gave Miriam a big hug.

Let's talk: Why didn't Miriam want to give Lacey a present? What did Mom tell her? What kind of giver does God love? What special reason do we have for giving cheerfully to others? Why did Miriam's mom hug her?

Older children and adults may read: 2 Corinthians 9:6–8

Let's pray: Dear Lord Jesus, please keep us from being selfish with what we have. Help us to be thankful that You gave Your life for us and still give us everything we need. Make us willing to show our thanks by being cheerful givers, especially to those who need help. Amen.

I delight to do [Your] will, O my God. Psalm 40:8 (RSV)

A Good Way to Have Fun

A rich man was feeling sad. He thought he was sick, so he went to a doctor. The doctor guessed what was really wrong. He said, "Take $10,000 and visit those in need this week. Buy them what you think they need, and help them in any way you can."

The rich man did this. The next week he went back to the doctor and said, "I never had so much fun in my life. It was the best medicine I could have taken." He was right. You will enjoy doing good and helping the poor and needy.

Some people might think that Jesus was always sad, but most of the time He was very happy. He enjoyed helping people. He enjoyed being with people at weddings and dinners. He enjoyed teaching them God's Word. He even was glad to suffer and die for all of us. He did all this to save us from our sins.

Jesus loved doing what His heavenly Father wanted Him to do. Can you say, "I enjoy doing whatever You want me to do, O my God?" Are you glad to do God's will? His Holy Spirit will help you do it.

Let's talk: What do you think was wrong with the rich man? How did he forget his troubles and become happy? Was Jesus happy when He helped people? What was Jesus glad to do for all of us? Why did Jesus enjoy doing what our Father in heaven wanted Him to do? When do we gladly obey God?

Older children and adults may read: Psalm 40:1–3, 7–8

Let's pray: Dear Father in heaven, we want to enjoy doing Your will as Jesus did when He lived on earth. Often we don't obey You; please forgive us for Jesus' sake. Help us love You more so that we will enjoy doing whatever You want us to do. Amen.

Come, all you who are thirsty, come to the waters; and you who have no money, come, buy and eat! Isaiah 55:1

God's Gifts Are Free

Imagine a young boy standing across from a big grocery store. In the front windows are heaps of apples and oranges and other fruit. Inside are bread and milk and lots of other food. The little boy hasn't eaten all day. He does not have any money.

Then the man who sells all those good things comes out of the store. He waves to the boy and other people who are passing by. He says, "Hey, everyone who is thirsty, come and get a free drink; and if you have no money, come anyway and buy and eat!"

The boy can't believe it! But he is thirsty and hungry, and it sounds good; so he runs over and says that he would like some milk. "I don't have any money," he says.

The man gladly gives him all the milk he wants.

Then the boy points to some bananas, and the man sticks three in the boy's pocket. The man also gives the boy a loaf of bread, some cookies, a quart of ice cream, and all the apples he can carry.

That isn't what most store owners would do. But it is what God does. One day God's prophet Isaiah said, "Come, all you who are thirsty, come to the waters; and you who have no money, come, buy and eat." Isaiah was thinking of the good things God has for us and how we can have these good things without paying for them. In the Bible, God invites everybody to come and enjoy His gifts without paying for them.

Do you know what the water and bread are that God wants us to buy from Him without money? His love and the forgiveness of all our sins. For Jesus' sake, God wants to give us His love free—for nothing! All we need to do is believe what He has told us in the Bible. It's almost too good to believe, isn't it?

Let's talk: How do you think the hungry boy felt when he was given free food? What are the bread and water that God wants us to have? How much do we have to pay for God's love? Who may have God's love and blessings? How can anyone get God's gifts without paying for them?

Older children and adults may read: Isaiah 55:1–3

Let's pray: Dear Father in heaven, how glad we are that You are willing to give Your love to everyone free of charge. Give us Your Holy Spirit so that we will take Your gifts and have life with You forever. We ask this in the name of Jesus, our Savior. Amen.

He who is slow to anger is better than the mighty.
Proverbs 16:32 (RSV)

The Better Way

Mr. Kessner rushed up to Mrs. Morrow's door and pounded on it. He hardly gave her time to open it before he started to complain. Mr. Kessner lived across the street in the big house with the wide lawn.

"I don't want your children running all over my lawn and ruining my flowers," shouted Mr. Kessner. "I knew when you moved in that you weren't much good. I try to keep my lawn looking good, but when people like you move in who don't care how things look, it's not long before my property looks bad too."

"When did my children run through your yard?" asked Mrs. Morrow.

"Don't act so innocent," sneered Mr. Kessner. "You know good and well it happened yesterday afternoon. You probably told them to do it."

"But we weren't home at all yesterday," said Mrs. Morrow. "I took the children to my mother's house early in the morning, and we came back well after dark."

"Oh," said Mr. Kessner in a very quiet voice. "Well, see that your children stay off of my lawn."

After Mr. Kessner left, Mrs. Morrow sat quietly in the living room, gathering her thoughts. Her husband came into the room and asked what all the shouting had been about. Mrs. Morrow explained the visit from Mr. Kessner.

Mr. Morrow said. "I'm afraid I would have yelled back at Mr. Kessner. You acted the way Jesus would want you to act."

The next morning, a bouquet of fresh-cut flowers was on the Morrow's front porch with a note from Mr. Kessner. He said he was sorry for his behavior.

Let's talk: Why was Mr. Kessner angry? Did Mrs. Morrow get angry? What might have happened if Mrs. Morrow had gotten angry, too? What makes it hard to keep from getting angry and hateful? Which is better—to act big and tough or to be kind and gentle? Why? Memorize the Bible verse.

Older children and adults may read: Proverbs 16:27–30

A poem to remember:
Christ is kind and gentle;
   Christ is pure and true.
And His own dear children
   Follow that way, too.

Let's pray: Dear Jesus, please help us be slow to get angry. Remind us that we are to treat others as we want to be treated. Thank you for forgiving us when we do yell at others and accuse others of things they haven't done. In Your name. Amen.

My command is this: Love each other as I have loved you.
John 15:12

Something Jesus Wants Very Much

"I told you twice to pick up your clothes," Mom said to her son, Joel. She shouldn't have to tell him twice, should she?

There's something Jesus told His disciples twice. That must mean He really wants us to do it. Jesus said "Love each other" two times in one conversation. In between Jesus said, "You are My friends if you do what I command."

Why did Jesus say "Love each other" twice? Perhaps because Peter would sometimes get angry with Philip, or Nathanael would argue with Thomas. Sometimes the disciples were even jealous of one another. They needed to be told twice.

We often argue with one another at home or at school. We get angry very easily. We say bad words to each other. Sometimes we even hit or kick or do other mean things. Do you know what Jesus wants us to do? He said, "My command is this: Love each other as I have loved you."

How much did Jesus love us? So much that He died for us on the cross. That's how much we should love one another. That's quite a lot, isn't it? Would you be willing to die for someone else? Jesus died for all people. He died to save us from our sins. He wants us to love the way He loved us.

Let's talk: What is the command Jesus gave to His disciples? Why do you think Jesus said these words twice? Who needs to remember that God wants His children to love one another? How much should we love one another? How much has Jesus loved us?

Older children and adults may read: John 15:12–17

Let's pray: Dear Lord Jesus, we're sorry that we haven't loved one another as much as we should. Please forgive us and help us to love others as You have loved us. In Your name we pray. Amen.

Jesus [said], "Don't be afraid; just believe." Mark 5:36

Never Be Afraid

When the man left his daughter, she was very sick. The man went to Jesus and begged Him to help her. Then somebody came and told the father, "Your daughter is dead. Don't bother Jesus anymore."

Jesus heard what was said. He saw the father get white in the face. The father thought Jesus couldn't help him now. So Jesus put His hand on the man's shoulder and said, "Don't be afraid; just believe."

Together they went to the man's home. Jesus made the girl alive again. She wasn't even sick anymore.

Jesus can help when nobody else can. Jesus can help even when nobody thinks He can. All we have to do is trust Him to help us.

If you're in trouble, don't forget Jesus. He loves all people just as much today as He did when He was on earth. And He is just as strong. He can help you, and He wants to help you, so that you never need to be afraid.

Let's talk: What did the father ask Jesus to do? What did someone come and tell the father? Why did the father become afraid? What did Jesus say? What did Jesus do?

Why can Jesus help us in any kind of trouble? Because we believe in Jesus, why don't we ever have to be afraid? Memorize the Bible verse.

Older children and adults may read: Mark 5:35–43

Let's pray: Dear Jesus, we believe that You are the Son of God and our loving Savior. Please help us trust in You at all times. Then we won't be afraid of anything, even death, because You give people a life that never ends. Amen.

As high as the heavens are above the earth, so great is His love for those who fear Him. Psalm 103:11

The Greatness of God's Love

Derek asked his father, "How big is the sun?"

His father, who was a farmer, answered, "Oh, the sun's maybe as big as a load of hay."

"That's pretty big," said Derek. "It doesn't look that big."

The sun is actually much bigger than a load of hay. It's bigger than the whole earth—much bigger. We can't see how big the sun really is. We can't even imagine how big it is.

How big is the love of God? It, too, is much bigger than we think. As high as the heavens are above the earth, higher than anybody could climb or fly or see, that's how big God's love is for those who fear Him. If God's love were like a tree growing straight up, nobody could ever find the top of it. The Bible says God's love doesn't have an end.

God's love is for those who fear Him. Who fears God? The word *fear* in this sentence doesn't mean to be *afraid* of God. It means to love God and be afraid of sin. And those who fear God and are sorry for their sins discover that God's love is very great—always big enough to forgive them.

Let's talk: How big did Derek's father say the sun was? How big is the sun, really? How big does the psalmist say God's love is? Whom does God love in a great big way? Who fears God in the right way? What will we be afraid to do because we love God? What does God always do for Jesus' sake?

Older children and adults may read: Psalm 103:8–13

Let's pray: How wonderful is Your love, dear God, and how great! Help us fear You in the right way—to love You so much that we will never want to sin. When we do sin, please forgive us for Jesus' sake. Amen.

A friend loves at all times. Proverbs 17:17

How to Have Good Friends

"I hate Monique. She said my hair looks funny," Angela grumbled, a frown causing her lower lip to stick out.

Kevin, Angela's big brother, looked at her with a confused expression. "I thought Monique was your friend," he said.

"She's not my friend if she says mean things to me," said Angela.

"Maybe you're not a good friend either if you get angry at Monique," said Kevin. "Do you remember the Bible verse you learned about friendship?"

"Which one?" Angela asked.

"The one that says, 'A friend loves at all times,' " Kevin said.

Angela remembered. She had learned it in Sunday school. "Oh, sure. 'A friend loves at all times,' " Angela said without much enthusiasm.

"When Monique said your hair looked funny, you could have said, 'Does it? Why do you think it looks funny?' Then maybe you'd still be good friends," Kevin told his sister.

"I guess I'm the one who wasn't a good friend 'cause I stopped loving Monique," Angela admitted.

"Now you're on the right track," said Kevin. "You're not a very good friend if you get angry easily. A real friend loves at all times. Just think of how Jesus loves us at all times. That's why He's called the best Friend anyone ever had."

"You know what, Kevin? I don't hate Monique anymore," Angela said with a grin. "I want to keep on being her friend."

Let's talk: Why did Angela say she hated Monique? What Bible verse did Kevin tell her? Why wasn't Angela being a good friend? Who is the best Friend anyone ever had? What is Jesus willing to do for us at all times?

Older children and adults may read: Proverbs 17:13–17

Let's pray: Dear Father in heaven, please help us to be good friends, ones who don't quit being friends over little things. Help us to be the kind of friend Jesus always is to us. We ask this as His children. Amen.

I am … wonderfully made. Psalm 139:14

Your Wonderful Body

Manuel cut his finger on a can. He ran into the house. His mom had Manuel hold his finger under the faucet while she looked for a Band-Aid.

"Why does my finger bleed?" asked Manuel.

"Because God wants the blood to wash the place where you cut yourself," answered Mother. "The can was dirty. We'll clean the cut with medicine, but the blood washes it, too."

After a while Manuel said, "It's stopped bleeding now."

"That's good," said Mother. "Now the blood will cover the cut. Then new skin will start to grow under the dry blood."

"God makes the blood work that way, doesn't He?" asked Manuel.

"The Bible says, 'The Lord made us.' In another place, it says, 'I am fearfully and wonderfully made.' God made each and every part of us, and He even made blood so it could clean cuts," Mother answered.

"You know what else is wonderful? Fingernails! When my nail came off last year, it hurt to grab things. Now I have a new fingernail," Manuel said with a smile.

"And your eyes are wonderful, and your hands, and your tongue, and your toes," said Mother as she hugged Manuel.

"That's 'cause God made me," said Manuel.

Let's talk: Can you think of anything that is more wonderfully made than you are? Who made you? What wonderful things have you noticed about your body? If someone loses a hand, can the hand be replaced? Will it be as good as the one God gave you? Because God made you, to whom do you belong? What are some ways of thanking God for your body and for His love?

Older children and adults may read: Psalm 139:1–14

Let's pray: Thank You, dear heavenly Father, for giving us such wonderful bodies. Help us take care of them and teach us to please You in whatever we do, for Jesus' sake. Amen.

The Lord has done great things for us, and we are filled with joy. Psalm 126:3

Why Christians Are Glad

"Oh, boy, isn't this a nice home!" said Shane. His family's old house had burned down, and they were moving into a new one. He ran upstairs to put the first piece of furniture into *his* room. In this new house, he had a room all to himself. And Shane wasn't the only one who was happy—his whole family was excited about the new house.

That night, when everything was unloaded and just before it was time to eat, Shane's father said, "Let's all sit down in the living room and thank God for doing so much for us. He took care of us when our old house burned down; and now He's even given us a better house than the one we had."

After everyone had gathered in the living room, Shane's father read Psalm 126. He explained that it's a song that praises God for letting His people return home after some enemies had captured them and taken them far away.

"I think we should all remember a verse from that psalm," Shane's mom said. "It will help us remain thankful for what God has done for us."

"I know what verse you mean," said Shane. "It's the part that says, 'The Lord has done great things for us, and we are filled with joy.' It's true, too."

The whole family said the verse together. Then Shane's father led them in prayer. "Thank You, dear Lord, for making us God's children, for watching over us, for blessing us with a new home," Shane's father prayed. "Help us to be thankful always. Amen."

Let's talk: What happened to Shane's old house? Why was Shane happy? What did Shane and his family do before supper? Which psalm did Shane's father read? What verse did Shane's mother want them to memorize? What great things has the Lord done for us? Has He done anything special for your family?

Older children and adults may read: Psalm 126

Let's pray: Dear Lord Jesus, You have done so many great and good things for us. We're glad that we're Your children. Help us show our thanks in all that we do and keep us in Your love. In Your name we pray. Amen.

Whoever wants to become great among you must be your servant. Matthew 20:26

How to Become Great

Mr. Ritter could hear the children fighting in the back yard. Each one was shouting, "Me first!" No one wanted to be second. Mr. Ritter took some popcorn out to the kids. While they ate, he told them this Bible story:

> The helpers of Jesus, the 12 disciples, started fighting one day. Every disciple thought he should be in charge. When Jesus heard about this, He called His friends together and said, "Some people try to rule other people, but you must not be that way. Whoever wants to be great among you must be your servant."

Jesus also told His disciples that He didn't come to be served, but to serve and to give His life for other people. Jesus showed His friends and helpers how to be like Him.

After he explained the story, Mr. Ritter asked, "Who is the better player—the one who always wants to bat or pitch, or the one who will play where the team needs the most help?"

All the children answered, "The one who will play where the team needs the most help."

"It's like that in everything else, too," said Mr. Ritter. "Jesus knew where we needed the most help—we needed to be forgiven for our sins. So He died and rose again for us. He wants us to be helpful and serve others also."

Let's talk: Why were the children fighting? What Bible story did Mr. Ritter tell them? Who is the best ball player? How do Jesus' friends become great? What did Jesus give up to help all people?

Older children and adults may read: Matthew 20:20–28

Let's pray: Dear Lord Jesus, forgive us when we try to be important by pushing other people around. Help us remember that You want us to become great by serving others. We're thankful that You were willing to die for us, and we love You for it. Amen.

Let another praise you, and not your own mouth.
Proverbs 27:2

Don't Blow Your Own Horn

Jesus once told a story to people who thought they were better than others. It was about a Pharisee and a Publican. Both men were in the temple praying.

The Pharisee's prayer went something like this:

"I thank You, God, that I am better than other people, better than cheaters, better than unfair people, or people who aren't decent. I do more good things than I have to. I often go without eating. And I give God 10 cents out of every dollar I get."

That was what the Pharisee said. But God didn't like his prayer. It wasn't really a prayer at all. He was just telling God what a good man he was. He was praising himself. He was bragging.

God doesn't want us to say how good we are. The Bible says, "Let another praise you, and not your own mouth." When we praise ourselves, we are proud. When we think we're better than someone else, we forget that we are all sinners.

But when other people praise us, we can feel good about it. They'll notice what we do without our telling them. And even when others don't appreciate what we're doing, Jesus will.

Let's talk: How did the Pharisee pray? Why wasn't this a prayer? What would Jesus rather have us say in our prayers? Why doesn't God want people to praise themselves? Who will praise us when we do good?

Older children and adults may read: Luke 18:9–14

Let's pray: Dear Father in heaven, we know we're sinners. We're far from being what You want us to be. Please forgive our sins for Jesus' sake. Make us more like Him so that others will see our good works and praise You for them. We ask this in Jesus' name. Amen.

The Lord knows those who are His. 2 Timothy 2:19

God Can See Who Believes

Everybody in Hope Church was talking. Adults were shaking their heads. The president of the church hadn't paid enough taxes to the government. He had to go to jail.

"Mr. Keiler was a bad man, wasn't he?" asked Alexis.

"Let's just say he was a sinner," answered her father. "But we're all sinners."

"But Mr. Keiler can't go to heaven if he cheated, can he?" Alexis asked.

"Can someone who hits another person expect to be in heaven?" asked Father. Alexis hung her head. She had hit her younger sister that morning.

Then Alexis remembered something from Sunday school. "Jesus died for Mr. Keiler's sins, even something as bad as cheating the government. All Mr. Keiler has to do is say he's sorry for what he did wrong, and Jesus will forgive him," said Alexis. "Then he can."

"Can what?" asked Father.

"Mr. Keiler can go to heaven," said Alexis. "Because God forgives all our sins for Jesus' sake, we get to go to heaven, right?"

Alexis' father was surprised at how much she knew about God and His love for all people. "You're right," he answered. "God so loved the world that He gave us His only Son, Jesus, to be our Savior. Whoever believes in Him will not die but will live with God in heaven always. Maybe Mr. Keiler has already asked God to forgive him."

"How do we know who believes in Jesus?" Alexis asked with a perplexed look on her face. "Maybe some people just say they believe."

"God knows. In fact, the Bible says, 'The Lord knows

those who are His,' " Father explained. "He knows whether you trust in Jesus as your Savior. You can't fool Him."

∽

Let's talk: Why did the president of Hope Church go to jail? Why could he still go to heaven? Was Alexis a sinner, too? For how many people did Jesus die on the cross? Why? Who receives forgiveness of sins from God? Who knows whether a person really believes in Jesus? Memorize the Bible verse.

Older children and adults may read: 2 Timothy 2:15–19

Let's pray: Dear Lord, we want to belong to You. Please keep us from sin. And when we sin, please forgive us. Help us always believe that You died on the cross for all sinners, including ourselves. Please let us all be in heaven with You someday because of Your love. Amen.

Dear children, let us not love with words or tongue but with actions and in truth. 1 John 3:18

Talk Is Cheap

"I love you, Mom," said Emily. "I love you more than my tongue can tell."

Then Emily went out to play and left Mom to load the dishwasher. That was something Emily could have done for her mother.

"I love my dad," Tyler said. But when he heard Dad mowing the lawn, Tyler hid in his room until the job was done. He didn't want to help.

"I love Jesus," some people say. But they aren't willing to follow in His footsteps. They aren't willing to love others as He loved us.

You may say, "I love other people," but if you have something someone needs and you don't give it to that person, do you really love that person? Or if you can help someone and you don't, are you loving the way God loves us?

It's easy to say, "I love you," isn't it? It's easy to say, "I love Jesus." But people who really love others show their love, not only by what they say but also by what they do. The apostle John said, "Dear children, let us not love with words or tongue but with actions and in truth." Words aren't true unless they are proved by actions.

Let's talk: What did Emily say to her mother? What did she do? What did Tyler say? What did he do? How do we show that we love Jesus? What shows that we don't love others even when we say we do? Memorize the Bible verse.

Older children and adults may read: 1 John 3:16–18

Let's pray: Dear Lord, forgive us for not always showing our love for others with actions. Help us show that we really love You and others by what we do and not just by what we say. In Jesus' name. Amen.

Do not say, "I'll do to him as he has done to me."
Proverbs 24:29

Take No Revenge

"When I get John, I'll give him two black eyes," Corey shouted as he slammed his right fist into his left hand.

"Why? What happened?" Dad asked.

"John hit me in the eye with his elbow," Corey said, pointing to a small bruise under his right eye.

"I'm sorry you got hit," said Dad. "John probably didn't mean to hit you with his elbow though."

"It still hurts," answered Corey with a pout.

"It probably does," said Dad. "So now you want to give John *two* black eyes? If you did that, what do you think John would want to do to you?"

"Probably hurt me worse," answered Corey.

"And so it could keep on going. Each time somebody would hurt the other one worse than before. Do you think it would be a good idea to let that go on for a month?"

"No, I guess not," said Corey.

"How can you stop it from going on?" Dad asked.

"Well, I guess I just won't hit him at all," Corey said. That was a much better plan than Corey's first answer to the situation.

The Bible says, "Do not say, 'I'll do to him as he has done to me.'" Jesus prayed even for those who nailed Him to the cross. He said, "Father, forgive them." Jesus forgives everybody's sins.

Christians may defend themselves, but God's Word says, "Don't say, 'I'll do to him as he has done to me.'" Jesus showed us something better than getting even. He told us to turn the other cheek.

Let's talk: Why was Corey angry? What could have happened if Corey had gotten even with John? Does it make things better or worse to hit someone back? What's the difference between defending ourselves and taking revenge? How did Jesus treat those who nailed Him to the cross? Because Jesus' lives in us, how can we treat others?

Older children and adults may read: Matthew 5:38–41

Let's pray: Heavenly Father, help us avoid saying, "I'll treat others the way they treat me." Help us love those who hurt us, the way Jesus did. In Jesus' name we ask this. Amen.

Praise the Lord, O my soul. Psalm 103:1

What Your Soul Should Do

Do you know what kind of song book Jesus used? He used the book of Psalms. The psalms are poems. Many of these poems were sung as hymns. One of them begins and ends with these words: "Praise the Lord, O my soul." What do you think that means?

"Praise the Lord" means we should give God all the honor and glory and thanks He deserves. The psalm tells why we want to thank and praise God. The main reason is that He forgives all our sins and loves us and provides everything we need.

Who should praise the Lord? The psalm says that our souls should. What is the "soul"? Suppose a dollmaker made a doll just as big as you, one that looked just like you. What would the difference be between you and the doll? The doll isn't alive. It has no soul.

My soul is me while I'm alive; your soul is you while you're alive. When the psalm writer said, "Praise the Lord, O my soul," he meant that he would thank and praise the Lord with his whole heart and life.

Jesus deserves to be thanked and praised. He saved us from being punished for our sins. He died for us on the cross and rose from the grave so that God can forgive all our sins. He loves us as a father loves his children. And someday He will take us to heaven. "Praise the Lord, O my soul."

Let's talk: What are the psalms? What are the words at the beginning and end of Psalm 103? What does "Praise the Lord" mean? What is our "soul"? Why do we want to praise Jesus? How can we thank and praise Him with our whole life?

Older children and adults may read: Psalm 103:1–5

Let's pray: We thank and praise You, Lord Jesus, for all that You have done for us and still do for us. We especially thank You for loving and forgiving us every day. Please help us show that we're thankful by the way we act. In Your name. Amen.

The Lord knows the thoughts of man. Psalm 94:11

God Knows What You Think

"Mom, why does God go by what we think in our hearts?" Anne asked one day.

"You would, too, if you could," said Mom.

"I would?" asked Anne.

"I think so," said Mom. "If somebody invited you to a party, and you knew she was thinking, 'I hope Anne stays away,' would you go?"

"No, I wouldn't go if they didn't want me," answered Anne.

"And if somebody said, 'You look lovely, Anne,' but you knew that he was really laughing at you inside, would you be happy about what he said or sad over what he thought?" Mom asked.

"I wouldn't feel so good," said Anne.

"That's why I think we would all go by what people think if we could," Mom explained. "The only problem is we can't always see what they think. But God can. He knows just what we are and how we feel and what we really mean. He knows that we are often selfish and proud and foolish."

God also knows when we are sorry for our sins. He knows if we really believe that Jesus died and rose again to save us. He forgives our bad thoughts and actions and is happy because we love Jesus.

Let's talk: What kind of wrong thoughts do we often have? Does God go by what we think or by what we say? What kind of thoughts does God want us to have? What does He do with our bad thoughts and actions because of Jesus?

Older children and adults may read: Psalm 94:9–12

Let's pray: Dear God, we know we can hide nothing from You. Please forgive all our sins for Jesus' sake. Keep us from bad thoughts and actions and teach us to obey You in all things. In our Savior's name. Amen.

Love your enemies and pray for those who persecute you.
Matthew 5:44

How to Treat Mean Children

"Mom, I'm never going to play with Anissa again. She's soooooo bad," Mikki said.

"That doesn't sound like it came from the mouth of someone who loves Jesus," said Mom.

"But you don't know how much Anissa hates me," replied Mikki. "Every day she's mean to me. She's always hitting me when nobody is looking, and then she says she didn't do it."

"What have you tried to do to help yourself?" asked Mom.

"What can I do? She's bigger than me," Mikki said with tears in her eyes.

"Have you tried what Jesus said we should do?" asked Mom.

Mikki thought for a minute. "What did He say?" she asked.

"Jesus said, 'Love your enemies and pray for those who persecute you.' Why don't you try that?" Mom said.

Mikki gave it a try. She knew Anissa collected stamps, so she hunted for a special stamp and gave it to Anissa. Mikki also told Anissa how pretty her smile was. Every night Mikki included Anissa in her prayers.

Pretty soon Anissa was nice to Mikki, and they became friends. One Sunday Mikki took Anissa to church. The two friends went to church together every Sunday after that. When Anissa learned about Jesus, she told Mikki, "Now I know why you were nice to me even when I wasn't nice to you."

Let's talk: Why didn't Mikki like Anissa at first? What did her mom say? What did Mikki try? How did it turn out? Memorize the Bible verse.

Older children and adults may read: Matthew 5:43–48

Let's pray: Dear Jesus, please help us love our enemies as You loved us. Even when children hate us and are mean to us, remind us to love them for Your sake. Amen.

Find out what pleases the Lord. Ephesians 5:10

The Best Lesson of All

"No more homework for a whole week," said Tamarcus with a huge smile on his face. It was time for Easter vacation.

"Then this week you can learn the best lesson of all," his dad replied.

"Oh, Dad, another lesson?" grumbled Tamarcus.

"It's an easy lesson to learn, but a hard one to do," said Dad.

"What's the lesson?" Tamarcus asked, his curiosity getting the better of him.

"It's in the Bible," answered Dad. "In Paul's letter to the Ephesians, he writes, 'Find out what pleases the Lord.' "

" 'Find out what pleases the Lord.' Is that the lesson?" asked Tamarcus. "I already know that."

"Don't be so sure," Dad said. "Does your mouth always know what pleases Jesus? Do your eyes? Do your hands? Do they know it so well that they do it? It's not enough to know what is right and true. God wants us to *do* what pleases Him."

Let's talk: Which lesson did Tamarcus' father want him to learn? Why did Tamarcus think he knew the lesson? Did Tamarcus still have to learn the lesson? Why do we? Memorize the Bible verse.

Older children and adults may read: Ephesians 5:1–10

Let's pray: Dear God, please help us find out what pleases You. Make us glad and able to do it. In Jesus' name we ask this. Amen.

Your Word is a lamp to my feet. Psalm 119:105

The Best Flashlight

"Mom, it's dark outside," Kathy said. "I can't see, and I want to go to the garage." She'd left her library book in the car.

"Take this flashlight," said Mom. "It will show you the way."

Kathy used the flashlight, and it was easy to see the way. She could also see where not to go. Wherever she pointed the flashlight, the light showed the path in front of her. It helped her get to the garage and safely back to the house.

"What do you think is the best flashlight in the world?" Kathy's father asked when she came back. "I'll give you a hint, it's called a lamp instead of a flashlight."

"I know," said Kathy. " 'Your Word is a lamp to my feet and a light for my path.' King David said that."

"That's right," said Dad. "In the days when King David lived, people didn't have flashlights. They had little oil lamps that they carried when they went out in the dark. How is God's Word like a lamp or a flashlight?"

Kathy thought for awhile. "The flashlight helped me see the way in the dark," Kathy answered. "The light also kept me from falling over something and getting hurt. The Bible shows us things we should avoid, and it shows us the way to heaven."

"Right again," said Dad. "What does the Bible say is the only way to get to heaven?"

"That's easy," said Kathy. "We can only get to heaven by believing that Jesus is our Savior. The Bible says, 'Whoever believes and is baptized will be saved.' "

Let's talk: What are flashlights good for? What did King David use instead of a flashlight? What did King David call God's Word? How is God's Word like a lamp or flashlight? What is the only way to heaven? How does God's Word keep us from sinning? Memorize the Bible verse.

Older children and adults may read: Psalm 119:97–104

Let's pray: Dear Lord, we're glad that we have Your Word as a light to show us the way to heaven and a lamp to help us avoid sin. Please let it shine brightly for us, for Jesus' sake. Amen.

Pleasant words are a honeycomb, sweet to the soul and healing to the bones. Proverbs 16:24

Some Words Are like Medicine

"I'm a doctor," said Elaine. "Grandma said so."

"Why did she say you were a doctor?" her mom asked.

"Grandma said, 'When you come, it's like good medicine.' I tell her funny stories, and it makes her happy," answered Elaine.

"Maybe you are a good doctor for her," said Mom. "I know a Bible verse about pleasant words. It says that 'Pleasant words are a honeycomb, sweet to the soul and healing to the bones.'

"In another place," her mom continued, "the Bible says, 'A cheerful look brings joy to the heart,' and 'A cheerful heart is good medicine.' "

Pleasant words *are* like good medicine. When people feel sad and you say something friendly, it cheers them up and makes them feel better.

A grouchy woman was cleaning rooms in a motel. One of the guests told her, "I'm glad you keep things so clean. You do your work quickly, too."

The woman smiled. "I don't hear things like that very often," she said. For many weeks those words were like good medicine for her. They made her feel good.

Saying something pleasant to another person is one of the easiest ways to share Jesus' love with those around us.

Let's talk: Why did Grandma say that Elaine was a doctor? What do pleasant words do for a person? What does our Bible verse say about pleasant words? When is it hard to find pleasant words to say to other people? When is it easy? Why should we say pleasant words to others?

Older children and adults may read: Proverbs 16:23–29

Let's pray: Dear Father in heaven, Your words are like honey, sweet and good, and ours are often like vinegar. Help us make the hearts of other people glad by the things we say, especially by telling them about their Savior, Jesus. We ask this in His name. Amen.

Live a life of love, just as Christ loved us. Ephesians 5:2

How to Walk in Love

Kareem and Jacob were strolling down the street together. They started pushing each other off the sidewalk in fun. But soon Jacob began to get angry. He saw a new lawn a little farther down the street. It had just been planted and soaked with water, so it was muddy. As they walked past it, Jacob pushed Kareem into the mud.

Now Kareem became angry. He threw mud at Jacob. Jacob began to call his friend names. Kareem chased Jacob down the street, threatening to give him a black eye. The two boys weren't friends anymore.

If Jesus had been walking as a boy with Kareem and Jacob, what would He have done? Maybe He would have pushed playfully too. But He would have watched to see if His actions made His friends angry. And if anyone began to get angry, He would have stopped what He was doing. He would not have pushed Kareem into the mud.

What would Jesus do? That's a good question to ask as we walk through life. The Bible says, "Live a life of love, just as Christ loved us." Our whole life is a walk with Jesus to heaven. On the way, we sometimes forget to walk like Christians. We need to remember that Jesus is walking right beside us. We can ask Him to help us do the things He wants us to do.

"Live a life of love, just as Christ loved us," says the Bible. How did Jesus love us? Jesus gave up His life for us on the cross so God would forgive us and make us His children. When we love as Jesus has loved us, He helps us forget about ourselves and do things for others.

Let's talk: If Jesus had been with Kareem and Jacob, what would He have done? What happened when Kareem and Jacob stopped living in love? What does it mean to "live in love"? What has Jesus done for us? Why did He do it? Because of Jesus' love, how much can we love others?

Older children and adults may read: Ephesians 5:1–2

Let's pray: Dear Jesus, please walk with us every day on our way to heaven. Help us learn from You how to walk in love. Forgive us when we forget. We ask this as Your children and followers. Amen.

I will show you my faith by what I do. James 2:18

Let's See What You Believe

Mr. Wilkey came out of a bar, half drunk, and stumbled into his pastor. "Mr. Wilkey, do you think you're a Christian?" Pastor Link asked.

Mr. Wilkey got angry. He took off his coat and was going to fight Pastor Link. "I'll show you I'm a Christian," Mr. Wilkey said.

Is fighting a way to show others that you're a Christian? No, the more you fight, the less people will think you're a

Christian. Christians are people who believe in Jesus and love Him. They have faith in Jesus. They believe that He is their Lord and Savior. They trust in Him. Jesus lives in their hearts.

But how can you show your faith? How can you prove that you believe what you say you believe? How can you see whether other people have Jesus in their hearts?

James, one of Jesus' disciples, wrote in the Bible, "I will show you my faith by what I do." We show what we believe by what we do. Jesus said people will see that we are His disciples if we love one another.

Suppose you saw someone who didn't have enough clothes and had nothing to eat, and you had extra clothes and extra food. Suppose you said to that person, "I love you. I hope you get some clothes and food." If you didn't give that person anything, would he think you really loved him?

James said, "I will show you my faith by what I do." He meant that people will be able to see whether we really love them by what we do. And our actions also will show whether we love Jesus.

Let's talk: How was Mr. Wilkey going to show Pastor Link that he was a Christian? Why isn't that a good way to show that we love Jesus? What's a good way to show others that we're Jesus' followers?

Older children and adults may read: James 2:14–18

Let's pray: Lord Jesus, we believe that You are our God and our loving Savior. Forgive us for not always showing that we believe this. Help us show our faith in You through our actions. Help us show our love for You by helping others. In Your name. Amen.

Do not let any unwholesome talk come out of your mouths, but only what is helpful for building others up. Ephesians 4:29

Is Your Mouth Clean?

"Mary, what time is it?" asked her mom.

"Mmmmmmmmm" is all Mary said.

Mom turned around. "What on earth?" she said when she saw Mary's mouth taped shut.

Mary took off part of the tape so she could explain. "You said I should tape my mouth shut when I want to say bad words," Mary said.

They both laughed. "Did it keep you from saying something bad?" Mom asked.

"Yes, but it didn't keep me from thinking bad words," said Mary. "Bryce hid my doll again, and I felt like pulling out his hair and calling him names."

"The apostle Paul wrote in the Bible, 'Do not let any unwholesome talk come out of your mouths, but only what is helpful for building others up,' " said Mom. "I'm glad you tried to keep evil words from coming out of your mouth, but I'm afraid you need something besides tape."

"If I could stop *thinking* bad things, then I wouldn't *say* bad things, would I?" said Mary.

"That's right," said Mom, "And Jesus will help you avoid thinking bad thoughts and saying evil words."

↬

Let's talk: Why did Mary tape her mouth shut? Did it stop her from thinking bad words? Where do we need to stop bad words, at the mouth or in the heart? What Bible verse did Mary's mother tell her? Who will help us change our thoughts from bad to good?

Older children and adults may read: Ephesians 4:28–32

Let's pray: Dear Father in heaven, please forgive the many times when we have forgotten that we are Your children and have let mean or dirty words come out of our mouths. Make our hearts clean so that our words will build up instead of tear down. We ask this in Jesus' name. Amen.

You are forgiving and good, O Lord. Psalm 86:5

What God Is Ready to Do

Samantha had a horrible toothache. Her mom took her to the dentist before school. When Samantha and her mom walked into the dentist's office, the waiting room was full of people. "The dentist can't see you today," said the receptionist.

"But my tooth really hurts," said Samantha.

"Oh," said the receptionist, and she went and talked to the dentist. The dentist came to the door and told Samantha to come right in. "If you have a bad toothache, I'd better help you," she said with a smile.

That night Samantha told her older sister how nice the dentist was. "She helped me right away because I needed it," Samantha said.

"That's just the way God helps us all the time," said Monica. "He is always ready to forgive us."

"I'm glad we don't have to wait in a big waiting room every time we want God to forgive us," said Samantha.

"That's the truth," said Monica with a smile. "We need God's forgiveness every day. You know, the Lord is ready to forgive all who ask Him. He doesn't even wait to be asked. That's why King David was happy and said, 'You are forgiving and good, O Lord.' "

Let's talk: Why did Samantha think the dentist was nice? Why did King David call God good? Why do we need God's forgiveness every day? For whose sake is God ready to forgive us? How did Samantha feel when she thought about God's forgiveness? Memorize the Bible verse.

Older children and adults may read: Psalm 86:3–7

Let's pray: Dear Lord God, we're glad that You are always ready to forgive us—even before we come and ask You for mercy. Please forgive us all our sins this day. Keep us as Your children for Jesus' sake. Amen.

Go into your room, close the door, and pray to your Father who is unseen. Matthew 6:6

Places to Pray

"Mom, I found a great place to pray," said Daniel when he came home from school.

"Where?" Mom asked.

"On the bus," he answered with a grin. "When it's crowded with people, nobody pays any attention to you. I sat there and did what Pastor Hoffmann told us to do. I went around the world praying."

"How did you do that?" asked Mom.

"I thought about the missionaries in Japan and asked God to bless them. Then I hopped to Africa and the Philippines and Mexico and ..." Daniel said as he counted on his fingers.

"You did this on the crowded bus?" Mom asked in a surprised tone.

"Sure, I also pray when I'm delivering my papers," Daniel answered. "My Sunday school teacher told me that houses without Christians in them are in need of light. So when I know that the people in a house don't go to church, I ask Jesus to turn His light on in their house."

"Any place is a good place to pray," said Mom. "Jesus said we should shut our door and pray in secret. He meant we shouldn't show off when we pray. But we can talk to our Father in heaven all by ourselves, anywhere and any-time, without anybody knowing it."

Let's talk: How did Daniel pray around the world on the bus? Whom did Daniel pray for when he delivered papers? Why did Jesus tell us to pray in secret? Does God care where we pray? Where can you pray by yourself to God?

Older children and adults may read: Matthew 6:5–8

Let's pray: Dear heavenly Father, we're glad that we can talk to You any place at any time. Please keep us from showing off when we pray. Help us pray to You in our hearts even when we are all praying together. We ask this in Jesus' name. Amen.

The earth is full of [God's] unfailing love. Psalm 33:5

The Lord Is Love

"Isn't the grass pretty? God makes the grass green," Momma told Juan.

"Why does God make the grass green?" asked Juan.

"Because He loves us," Momma answered. "He also made the sky blue."

"Why did God make the sky blue?" asked Juan.

"You wouldn't like to have a purple sky or hot pink grass or black flowers or green snow, would you?" Momma asked.

The Bible says, "The earth is full of His unfailing love." Everything God has made in the world shows how much He loves us. When the sun starts to shine through the clouds on a cold day, we say, "How good the sun feels." Without the sun, nothing could live.

When the sun gets too hot and clouds cover it and it begins to rain, we say, "How good the rain is." God gives us the sunshine and the rain.

The easiest way to see that God loves us is to remember what Jesus did for us and what He promises us in the Bible. God sent His Son, Jesus, to die on the cross for all people. Because of that great love, we get to live as God's children.

Let's talk: What color would you choose for grass? Why did God make the world beautiful? What's so good about sunshine? Why does He send us rain? What are some other good things that God gives us because He loves us? What's the easiest way to tell that God loves us? Memorize the Bible verse.

Older children and adults may read: Psalm 33:1–8

Let's pray: Lord Jesus, our God and Savior, we thank and praise You for making the world and all that is in it. Thanks especially for the beautiful, bright colors. Most of all, we thank You for saving us and making us God's children. Amen.

You will be My witnesses. Acts 1:8

What Jesus Wants Us to Be

Have you ever seen a courtroom? A courtroom is a place where judges try to find out the truth about people the police catch.

There's a judge in a black gown who sits behind a table on a platform. There's the person who was arrested. There's a police officer. There's usually a witness or two to help tell about what happened. There are lawyers asking questions.

Jesus said that His followers should be like one of those five kinds of people. Do you know which one? Jesus didn't say we should be police officers, making sure people obey the rules. Jesus doesn't want us to be judges who punish people. Jesus didn't say we should be lawyers who question people. And He certainly doesn't want us to be people who break the rules.

Jesus said, "You will be My witnesses." Witnesses tell what they know. Some people believe them, some people don't, but that doesn't matter. Witnesses just tell what they know.

As His witnesses, what does Jesus want us to tell others? He wants us to tell people what we know about Him. He wants us to tell everyone that He died and rose again to save us from our sins. Some people we tell will believe; some won't. Whether they believe or not us not up to us. Only the Holy Spirit can work faith in a person's heart. Our job is to be witnesses for Jesus.

Have you ever told someone else about Jesus? Remember that Jesus wants you to be a witness for Him. Watch for a chance to speak up for Him every day.

Let's talk: What does a witness do in a courtroom? What did Jesus say we should be? When are we witnesses for Jesus? What could you tell about Jesus? Do you know anyone who needs to know about Jesus?

Older children and adults may read: Acts 1:7–9

Let's pray: Dear Jesus, please help us all learn more about You. Make us good witnesses for You. We want to tell others the truth about You. Help them to believe us. In Your name we ask this. Amen.

Now that you know these things, you will be blessed if you do them. John 13:17

Knowing and Doing

"I know the most Bible verses in my class," said Elizabeth. After a moment, she asked, "Mom, does that make me the best Christian in my class?"

Mom sat down next to Elizabeth. "I hope all the children in your class are good students and Christians," she said. "But knowing the most Bible verses doesn't make you the best Christian; in fact, it doesn't even make you Christian. Anyone can memorize words."

"But I learned them to make Jesus happy," Elizabeth explained.

"Then all the verses you memorized show that you love Jesus and that you want to be a faithful Christian," said Mom. "But there's a big difference between knowing and doing. What Bible verses do you know?"

Elizabeth said, "I know 'Trust in the Lord with all your heart' and 'Do not let your heart be troubled' and a lot more."

"Well, do you always remember that Jesus loves you and is with you all the time, and do you always trust that He can and will take care of you?" Mom asked.

"N-no, not always," Elizabeth admitted. "I still worry a lot, don't I?"

"I'm afraid so," said Mom with a smile. "What other verses do you know?"

"I know 'This is My command, that you love one another as I have loved you.' Jesus said that," Elizabeth told her mother.

"I'm glad you know that verse," said Mom. "But how about the doing? Do you always love Bradley the way Jesus loves you?" Mom knew that would be a hard question to answer because Elizabeth and her brother, Bradley, often fought.

"No, Mom," said Elizabeth. "I guess just knowing Bible verses doesn't make me a good Christian. But God will help me do what the verses say, won't He?"

"Yes," said Mom. "And Jesus said, 'Now that you know these things, you will be blessed if you do them.' He will give you all the help you need to be a good Christian and a happy one."

⁀

Let's talk: Was Elizabeth the best Christian because she knew the most Bible verses? Why not? What were some of the verses Elizabeth knew but didn't always do? What Bible verse do we know but don't always follow? What did Jesus say will make us happy?

Older children and adults may read: John 13:12–17

Let's pray: Dear Jesus, please help us learn the things You have taught. Help us also to do them. Amen.

The Lord our God is holy. Psalm 99:9

Our Holy God

"Holy, holy, holy, Lord God almighty" Jared and Jessica sang as loudly as they could. They were playing church on the porch steps. Jared was the preacher.

"I will now tell you why God is holy," Jared said to begin his sermon. But he didn't know how to continue. He ran inside to ask Mom.

"Mom, what's holy?" Jared asked.

"God is holy," Mom answered. "That means, God has no sin. God never does anything wrong. Everything God does is just right."

"Are you holy, Mom?" Jared asked.

"Oh, no," she replied with a laugh. "We all do things that we shouldn't do, and often we don't do what we should do. But God always does only what is right. He's holy. He's perfect."

"God's angels are holy," said Jared, remembering what he had heard in Sunday school.

"Yes" said Mom, "but people aren't holy. They do wrong things. You sin, don't you? Because all people sin, they're not holy. They need God's forgiveness."

"But aren't we holy when God forgives us?" asked Jared.

"Yes, that's right," said Mom. "Jesus washes away all our sins and makes us holy. But only God is holy in everything He does."

Jared went outside to finish his sermon.

Let's talk: What were Jared and Jessica playing? What hymn were they singing? What does *holy* mean? Who else is holy besides God? What keeps us from being holy? Who makes people holy? How does God expect His holy children to act? Memorize the Bible verse.

Older children and adults may read: Isaiah 6:1–8

Let's pray: Dear heavenly Father, we're glad that You never do anything wrong and always do what's right. Please forgive all our sins for Jesus' sake. Give us the Holy Spirit so that we may do what you want us to do. We ask this in Jesus' name. Amen.

When I am afraid, I will trust in [God]. Psalm 56:3

What to Do When You're Afraid

William and Laurel had played at the park too long. Now it was getting dark, and they had to walk past a cemetery to get home. There were dead people buried in the cemetery. Their friend Jackie had told them there were ghosts in the cemetery.

William and Laurel were a little afraid.

"Mom told us there are no ghosts in the cemetery," said Laurel, but she wasn't sure. She started to cry.

"I know," said William, trying to act brave, "but when it's dark, everything looks so spooky. Maybe something is hiding in there."

"I know, let's ask Jesus to go with us," said Laurel. The two children stopped and folded their hands. Laurel said, "Dear Jesus, be with us on our way home." They started walking again.

"Because Jesus is with us, we don't have to be afraid," William said, feeling better.

"Jesus is with us all the time," Laurel said. "I guess that means we never have to be afraid. I'm glad He's always with us."

"So am I," agreed William.

Let's talk: Why were William and Laurel afraid? Why don't we ever have to be afraid? What does the Bible verse tell us to do?

Older children and adults may read: Psalm 56:3–4, 9–11

Let's pray: Dear Jesus, thank You for being with us and loving us and taking care of us all the time. Please help us trust in You always. Amen.

You are the light of the world. Matthew 5:14

Are You a Shining Example?

"Get the lamp, Daddy, the lights are out" called Benjiro. There was an old lamp in the front closet. There was oil in the lamp and a wick that burned and made light. Benjiro's dad put the lamp on the table, and it brightened up the whole room.

"You know, Benjiro," said Dad, "that lamp is kind of like the lamps Jesus used when He lived on earth. While it's not exactly the same, it reminds me of what Jesus said about His people being lights. Do you know the words I mean?"

"He said 'You are the light of the world,' " answered Benjiro. "Is that what you were thinking of?"

"Yes, that's the verse I mean," said Dad. "All those who know Jesus and believe He's their Savior are like lamps that provide light. These believers tell others about Jesus and show them the way to heaven. They also brighten up other people's lives by what they do."

Benjiro watched the lamp for awhile. "That isn't a very strong light. Look how it flickers," he said.

"That lamp is like most of us," said Dad. "We aren't very strong Christians on our own, so our light flickers. But Jesus has brought us together into churches, and He promises to be with us wherever we are. Because He's there, the light is stronger and brighter.

"So don't forget: You are the light of the world—you and all the people who believe in Jesus," Dad said.

Let's talk: How is a Christian like a lamp? What can Christians help other people see? Sometimes our light is brighter and stronger than at other times. What makes it brighter and stronger? Memorize the Bible verse.

Older children and adults may read: Matthew 5:14–16

Let's pray: Dear Lord Jesus, help us shine brightly as Christians in all that we say and do. We want others around us to see how loving You are. We want others to believe that You are their Savior and follow You. Amen.

The Lord is ... slow to anger, abounding in love. Psalm 103:8

Is God Slow?

Timothy watched the storm approach. Lightning bolts streaked across the sky. Sometimes they went so fast he couldn't see where they started or where they ended. "God sure can do things fast," said Timothy. "Look how fast He makes the lightning go."

"There's one thing God is slow about doing," said his dad. "The Bible says, 'The Lord is ... slow to anger.' Even though we sin every day, He doesn't fly off the handle at us. He doesn't punish us as we deserve. Instead, He's very patient with us. It takes Him a long time to get angry."

The Bible also tells us why God is slow to get angry. It's because He is so kind and full of love. "The Lord is ... abounding in love," writes the psalmist. That means He is full of mercy. For Jesus' sake, God doesn't punish us for the sins we do. Instead, God forgives us because Jesus took our punishment for us on the cross. And then He rose again on Easter.

How wonderfully good our God is. That is why the psalm writer also says, "Praise the Lord, O my soul ... praise His holy name."

Let's talk: What made Timothy think that God does things quickly? What is God slow to do? Why is the Lord slow to get angry? Why is it good that God is slow to get angry? For whose sake is He full of love and kind and forgiving? Memorize the Bible verse.

Older children and adults may read: Psalm 103:8–13

Let's pray: Dear Lord God, how glad we are that You are slow to anger and that You eagerly forgive our sins for Jesus' sake. Help us to be kind and forgiving to others and slow to get angry. We ask this in Jesus' name. Amen.

[Jesus said,] "I am the Good Shepherd." John 10:14

The Lord Is My Shepherd

Once there was a shepherd who had 100 sheep. One evening he counted them as they went through the gate into the sheep pen. Only 99 were there—one was missing! It must not have followed him home, which meant the lamb probably was lost in the dark woods.

The shepherd quickly closed the gate and left his helpers to watch the 99 sheep. He had to find the lost lamb before a wolf or lion caught it. The shepherd hurried to the places where the lamb had been that day. He called the lamb's name.

For awhile the shepherd heard nothing. Again and again he called. At last he heard a weak "baa." Before long the shepherd found the lamb, tangled up in some bushes. He carefully pulled the lamb out, but it couldn't walk—its leg was hurt. The shepherd carried the lamb home on his shoulders.

"Look," he called to his helpers as he came back, "I found the lamb that was lost." All his helpers were happy with him.

This is a story about a shepherd we know. Jesus is the shepherd in this story. And we are the sheep. Sometimes we are like the lost lamb. When we sin, we go down a wrong path away from God. But Jesus goes out and finds us. He brings us back to the sheep pen. He even carries us when we are too tired to walk on our own. He wants us all to be safe with Him. And He's very happy about all those who are saved.

"I am the Good Shepherd," Jesus said. Our Good Shepherd even gave His life for His sheep.

Let's talk: Why did the shepherd leave his 99 sheep? What happened to the missing lamb? How did the shepherd bring the lost lamb home? Why was the shepherd glad? Who is the shepherd Jesus was talking about? Who are Jesus' sheep? When are we like the lost lamb? Why is Jesus called "the Good Shepherd"?

Older children and adults may read: Luke 15:3–7

Let's pray: Dear Jesus, our Good Shepherd, we're glad that we are Your lambs. Please keep us close to You every day. If we become lost, please call us back to You. Keep us always with You here on earth so that we will be with You in heaven. Amen.

[Jesus said,] "Blessed are the merciful." Matthew 5:7

Feeling Sorry for Other People

"I feel so sorry for Mrs. Jacobs," said Madeleine. "She's very poor, and now she's in the hospital. Her children are home with their grandmother, but she has trouble cooking because of her arthritis. I'm not sure what she can really make them to eat."

"I'm glad you feel that way, Madeleine," said Mother. "Jesus said, 'Blessed are the merciful.' "

"Does merciful mean feeling sorry for others?" Madeleine asked.

"It means more than just feeling sorry," Mother said. "It means you feel sorry enough to do something about it."

"But what can we do?" asked Madeleine.

"We could start by making some spaghetti and taking it over to the children. Do you think they would like that?" asked Mother.

Madeleine nodded yes, so she and her mother made a pot of spaghetti. Madeleine made some garlic bread, and her mother made a salad. The two took the meal over to Mrs. Jacobs' house along with a loaf of bread, some soup, and a carton of eggs.

At supper that night, Madeleine's family discussed Mrs. Jacobs' problems. Madeleine's father said, "I think I'll write a note to everybody living around here. I'll tell them I'm coming Saturday to collect money to help Mrs. Jacobs."

When Madeleine's father talked to the neighbors, most of them were glad to help Mrs. Jacobs. They gave enough to pay for a lot of her hospital bill. When Madeleine and her father took the money to Mrs. Jacobs, she cried and thanked God for people who are merciful.

"Blessed are the merciful, for they will be shown mercy," Jesus said. Because we love Jesus, we can be kind and helpful to others. That makes us happy. And Jesus promises that we will receive mercy and love from God in return.

Let's talk: How did Madeleine show that she was merciful? What did she and her mother do for Mrs. Jacobs' children? What did Madeleine's father do to help Mrs. Jacobs? What do merciful people receive from God? Memorize the Bible verse.

Older children and adults may read: 1 John 3:16–18

Let's pray: Thank You, dear heavenly Father, for feeling sorry for us and sending Jesus to save us from our sins. Thank You for giving us so many things that we don't deserve. We especially thank You for forgiving our sins. Help us to be merciful to people as You are merciful to us. In Jesus' name we ask this. Amen.

The Lord will hear when I call to Him. Psalm 4:3

God Listens to His Children

Have you ever been in trouble, bad trouble, when you didn't know what to do?

King David had many troubles. Before he became king, David had to run away from King Saul, who was trying to kill him. Later David had to run away from Absalom, his own son. Absalom tried to get rid of his father so that he could be the king.

Usually our troubles come from our sins. When we tell a lie, when we break something, when we treat others unkindly, when we forget to do something, we get into trouble. Some of King David's troubles were his own fault too.

But sometimes we get into trouble even when we haven't done anything wrong. Maybe somebody gets sick, or we lose our money, or we trip and fall, or someone treats us unkindly. There are many different kinds of troubles in the world.

What can we do when we're in trouble? We can pray to God. We can say what King David said. He said, "Answer me when I call to You, O my righteous God. ... Be merciful to me and hear my prayer."

King David knew that God would help him. He said, "The Lord will hear when I call to Him." So he prayed to God often, and then he stopped worrying.

We know that God loves all people, especially His children. We, too, can say, "The Lord will hear when I call to Him." Remember to ask God for help when you're in trouble. He will help you for Jesus' sake.

Let's talk: What did King David believe the Lord would do for him? What kinds of troubles do children have sometimes? What kinds of troubles do grown-ups have? Why can we ask God for help in times of trouble? Why are we happier when we trust God?

Older children and adults may read: Psalm 4:3–8

Let's pray: Dear God, we're glad that You are willing to help us in any trouble. We thank You for Your promises to hear our prayers. We know that You will help us for the sake of Jesus, our Savior. Amen.

Trust in the Lord. Proverbs 3:5

Why Terrell Didn't Worry

"I don't know what we'll do this week," Terrell's father said at the supper table. "I won't get paid until Friday, and we don't have any money for food."

"Jesus can help us," said Terrell. "Jesus once made a boy's lunch feed a lot of people."

"You're right, Terrell," said Mother. "Let's ask Jesus to help us."

So Father led the family in this prayer: "Dear Jesus, please help us get enough food this week."

Later that evening the telephone rang. It was the man who owned the convenience store on the corner. "I wonder if you could use some cans of food," he said. The man knew that Terrell's family was very big.

"I had some cans outside and didn't notice that it started to rain," the store owner said. "The labels came off the cans, and I don't know what's in them. I can't sell them like that. Could you use them?"

"Could I use them?" Father said excitedly. "You're the answer to my prayer."

"Trust in the Lord," said Mother when she learned about the store owner's offer. "Jesus always finds a way to help us when we depend on Him."

Terrell was right. Jesus always has a way to help us. There isn't anything that can keep Him from helping us. Sometimes He doesn't help us in a way we can see or understand. But He always knows the right way and the best time to help us.

We can always be sure that Jesus can and will help us. "Trust in the Lord," the Bible says. To trust means to believe that He will do what He has promised.

Let's talk: Why was Terrell's father worried? What did Terrell tell him? What happened when the family prayed to Jesus? Why doesn't Jesus always help right away? What does it mean to "trust in the Lord"?

Older children and adults may read: Proverbs 3:1–6

Let's pray: It's wonderful to know that we can always depend on You, dear Jesus. Please help us remember this, especially when we're in trouble. We thank You and love You for saving us from sin, our worst trouble. Keep us in Your kingdom and bless us. Amen.

My help comes from the Lord, the Maker of heaven and earth. Psalm 121:2

The Best Helper in the World

"Who helps God when He needs help?" Caleb asked his dad.

"God never needs help," Dad answered. "God can do anything. He's the almighty Maker of heaven and earth. If He needed anything, He could make it just by wanting it."

"Oh," said Caleb. After thinking a moment, he said, "Then God can always help us."

Caleb was right. Sometimes we ask our parents for something, but they can't help. When Caleb was sick, he asked his dad to help him get better. Caleb's dad could only give him medicine and stay with him until he felt better. But God made Caleb better. God can always help us. He can do anything. He made heaven and earth.

The Bible says, "My help comes from the Lord, the Maker of heaven and earth." Psalm 121 also says that the Lord never sleeps and that He watches over His children and keeps them from harm.

That's why the psalm writer said, "I lift up my eyes." He meant that he looked up to heaven—to God—for the help he needed. And he knew the Lord, who is in heaven, would help him.

⤳

Let's talk: What did Caleb ask his dad? Why doesn't God ever need help? Why can we be glad that our Helper is the Maker of heaven and earth? What did the psalm writer mean when he said he lifted up his eyes to the Lord? Why can we ask God to take care of us? Memorize the Bible verse.

Older children and adults may read: Psalm 121

Let's pray: Dear heavenly Father, we're glad that we are Your children. For Jesus' sake, love us and keep us with you. Teach us to trust in Your help. In Jesus' name. Amen.

Forget not all His benefits. Psalm 103:2

Reasons for Being Thankful

"Am I thankful!" Mrs. Andrews said. "My son was driving on Banner Road when he fell asleep and drove down a steep bank. The car rolled over twice, but he wasn't hurt. Isn't it wonderful how God kept him from harm?"

"Yes, it certainly is," said Miss Collier. "God certainly protected your son, but He keeps us from harm every day."

"How's that?" asked Mrs. Andrews.

"I drive on Banner Road at least 10 times a week," said Miss Collier. "I've never fallen asleep while driving. I've never run down the bank and never wrecked the car. Don't you think that's even more wonderful?"

Mrs. Andrews smiled. "I guess we forget about God's care until we have an accident like my son had," she said. "We really need to thank God when we don't have problems or accidents."

"Yes," said Miss Collier. "And the Bible says, 'Forget not all His benefits.' "

Let's talk: If a blind woman were able to see again, how would she feel? Would she be getting more blessings from God than we get? Why might she be more thankful for her eyes than we are? Do we thank God as much as we could?

What are some things that we can thank God for?

Older children and adults may read: Psalm 103:1–4

Let's pray: Thank You, dear Father in heaven, for all the love and care that You give us every day of our lives. Thank You for being so good to us even though we forget to thank You. Forgive us when we forget You. Keep us safe in Your love always, for Jesus' sake. Amen.

Even the winds and the waves obey Him! Matthew 8:27

Our Lord Is Mighty

A big storm blew across the lake. A strong wind whipped huge waves over the boat. Water poured into the boat faster than the men could scoop it out. Jesus was asleep at one end of the boat. His friends woke Him. "Lord, save us!" they said. They thought they were going to drown.

Jesus got up and talked to the wind and the water. He told them to be quiet. Right away the wind calmed down, and the water quit splashing. The friends of Jesus were surprised. They said, "What kind of man is this? Even the winds and the waves obey Him!"

Just think, Jesus can tell the wind to be quiet, and it quits blowing. He can tell the thunder to quit rolling or the rain to quit falling or the fire to quit burning or the sickness to quit hurting. Everything has to do what Jesus tells it to do.

If Jesus can make these things go away, why doesn't He chase away all our troubles? Often we don't ask Him to do so. And sometimes when we ask Him, He has a better plan or a better time to do what we ask.

A man once prayed to Jesus and asked Him to help him catch a plane. When the man arrived at the airport, the plane was gone. Later that day, the man learned the plane had crashed. The man was glad he'd missed the plane.

Jesus can do anything—He's God. Doctors said Sarah would never get better. Sarah said this prayer to Jesus: "I'm willing to be sick, if You want me to be sick, dear Jesus. But if it will be good for me, please make me well. The doctors don't think I can get better, but I know You can take away the sickness."

Jesus did make Sarah better. The doctors were surprised.

Let's talk: What was the wind doing on the lake? Who was in the boat? Why did they wake Jesus? What did Jesus tell the wind? What happened when Jesus told the wind to be still? What can Jesus say to our troubles? Why doesn't Jesus always take away our troubles? When will He take all our troubles away?

Older children and adults may read: Matthew 8:23–27

Let's pray: Dear Jesus, help us believe that You have power over all things. Teach us to pray to You in times of trouble. Because You know what's best for us, we ask that Your will be done and not ours. We know that You love us, and we love You. Amen.

"My thoughts are not your thoughts,"... declares the Lord.
Isaiah 55:8

The Best Thoughts

"I asked God for sunshine on my birthday, but it's raining," said Barry. "Why didn't God answer my prayer?"

"Barry, that question reminds me of a story," Mom said. "Two boys dug up some ground one day. One planted a garden, and the other collected some worms. That night the boy with the garden prayed for rain. The other boy prayed for sunshine so he could go fishing. What do you think God did?"

"I don't know," said Barry.

"Don't you think it would be better if we asked God for what we want and then be thankful for the answer He decides is best?" Mom asked. "Maybe other people needed rain on your birthday. God doesn't always think the way we think. He doesn't always do what we want, but His ways are always best."

" 'My thoughts are not your thoughts,' declares the Lord." He has much better thoughts than we do. We don't always forgive people who treat us unkindly. We get mad and maybe want to get even. Or we just quit being friends with that person.

But God thinks a lot differently than we do. He sent Jesus, His only Son, to die for our sins and rise again on the first Easter. Because of Jesus, God gladly forgives our sins. We can be glad that God doesn't think the way we do.

Let's talk: Whose ways of thinking are always better than ours? How do we think we should treat others who sin against us? What is God's way of treating us? For whose sake does He love us? Where can we find out what some of God's thoughts are? Memorize the Bible verse.

Older children and adults may read: Isaiah 55:6–9

Let's pray: Dear Father in heaven, forgive us for not always believing that what You do is best. We know that You love us and that all Your thoughts are good. Help us remember that we are Your dear children for Jesus' sake. Amen.

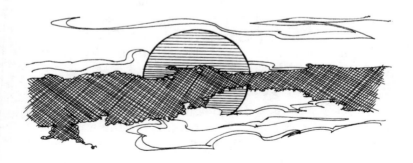

"If You are willing, You can make me clean." Mark 1:40

What Jesus Can Do for Us

When Jesus was alive, leprosy was something no one could heal. Persons with the disease had to leave home and live with others who had leprosy. They couldn't be around people who didn't have leprosy. People with the disease had to beg for food. Often they lived in caves or small huts and waited to die.

One day a man found out he had leprosy. He cried. Then someone came and told the man, "Jesus has been healing people with leprosy and has been doing many other wonderful things. People say that He's the Son of God and the Savior God promised to send."

The man with leprosy believed that Jesus could help him. He hoped Jesus would come to his town. Maybe Jesus would heal him. Otherwise he would never be healed.

One day the man heard that Jesus *was* coming to his town. The man stood as close to the town gate as he dared. He waited. At last Jesus came. There were a lot of people with Him. The man with leprosy ran to Jesus, nearer than the law said he could. He kneeled down in front of Jesus and said, "If You are willing, You can make me clean."

Jesus felt very sorry for the man. He even touched him. Nobody had touched him for a long time because people were afraid of catching leprosy. As Jesus touched him, He said, "I am willing. Be clean!"

Immediately the spots of leprosy were gone! The man's skin became smooth and clean, and he was healthy and strong again.

We don't have leprosy, but we do have something much worse—the sickness of sin. And no one can take away the sin in our hearts except Jesus. Like the man with leprosy, we can say to Jesus, "Lord, I'm sinful, but You can make me clean." Then Jesus says, "I forgive you; be clean!" Jesus washes away our sins. Then He helps us live a new life of faith in Him.

⁂

Let's talk: What disease did the man in the story have? What did he do when Jesus came to his town? What did he say to Jesus? What did Jesus tell the man with leprosy? What happened to the man's disease? What kind of sickness do we have? What can Jesus do for us? How do we know that He will help us?

Older children and adults may read: Mark 1:40–45

Let's pray: Dear Lord Jesus, we all have the sickness of sin, but You can make us clean. Take away all our sins so that someday we may be with You and all of God's children in heaven. Amen.

So in everything, do to others what you would have them do to you. Matthew 7:12

How to Treat Others

"You know what I wish?" Alika said to her mother. "I wish somebody would give me a whole pocketful of quarters." She liked candy bars, and she knew that they cost 50 cents.

"Do you know the Bible verse that's called the Golden Rule?" Alika's mother asked. "It says something about how you want others to treat you."

Alika knew the verse. "You mean the one that says, 'Whatever you want people to do to you, do that to them'? Does that mean I have to give away a pocketful of quarters to get more?"

"No, that Bible verse isn't really talking about quarters," said Mother. "Jesus was telling His disciples about how important it is to think of others first. That is one way we can share His love."

"I guess I was being selfish wanting a whole pocket of quarters all for myself," Alika said. "Maybe I could share the dollar I already have with Jennifer. She never gets to buy a candy bar."

"Now I think you know what that verse means," Mother said as she gave Alika a hug.

Let's talk: What did Alika wish for? What Bible verse did her mother ask her about? How does that verse tell us to treat other people? Who forgives us when we don't? Why? Memorize the Bible verse.

Older children and adults may read: Luke 6:30–35

Let's pray: Dear Jesus, we often want other people to do things for us, but we're not willing to do these things for others. Please forgive us for being selfish. Help us think about what will make other people happy. We ask this as Your dear children. Amen.

With [God] there is forgiveness. Psalm 130:4

Where to Get Forgiveness

Once there was a teacher who kept a little black book. In it she put a mark every time she saw a child do something wrong. Some of the children had a lot of marks in this book. At the end of each week, those who had marks were punished.

If God kept a book like that, how many marks do you think we would have? We'd have so many we couldn't count them. In a way, God does keep a book like that. He sees and remembers everything we do. The Bible calls God's memory a "book."

How do we get rid of the marks against us? There's only one way. The Bible says, "With God there is forgiveness." God sent His Son, Jesus, to take the punishment for all our black marks. He died on the cross and rose again. When Jesus did that, it was as if God erased all the marks by our names.

There is forgiveness with God—plenty of forgiveness for everybody's sins. Isn't that wonderful? Jesus paid for all the sins of everybody in the whole world. That's why there is forgiveness with God for every sin in the whole world.

Many people think they have done things that can't be forgiven. That isn't true. Judas betrayed Jesus, but he could have been forgiven. Pilate told the soldiers to nail Jesus to the cross. Was Jesus willing to forgive Pilate? Yes, He was. Peter said he didn't know Jesus. Did Jesus forgive him? Yes, He did. We've done many wrong things, too, and Jesus forgives us.

~

Let's talk: What did the teacher do? If God did that, how many marks would we have? What does God do with our marks? Why? How many sins will God forgive? Are any sins too bad to be forgiven? Why are we glad that God forgives every sin?

Older children and adults may read: Psalm 130:1–8

Let's pray: Dear Father in heaven, we believe that You forgive our sins just as You told us. That's why we're happy even though we have many marks against us. Thank You for sending Jesus to suffer and die for us. Help us do what is pleasing to You, for Jesus' sake. Amen.

A gentle answer turns away wrath. Proverbs 15:1

The Soft Answer

"Get out of here," Kyle yelled at his sister Lindsay. "You're an old cow."

"I sure am!" Lindsay replied. She tried to moo like a cow. Kyle laughed, and the argument stopped.

Lindsay knew that when someone is angry and says mean words, it doesn't make things better to shout back. It only makes the argument worse. Lindsay just smiled and said something nice or funny.

"A gentle answer turns away wrath," the Bible says. Wars have been started because leaders have said angry words instead of gentle ones.

At one time the people of Israel were about to fight against two of their own tribes. Those two tribes had built a large altar by the Jordan River similar to the altar in the tent church. The other 10 tribes of Israel thought these two tribes were starting their own religion.

Before fighting, the leaders of the 10 tribes sent some men to ask the two tribes why they weren't worshiping God anymore. The two tribes explained gently that they weren't worshiping another god. They were only trying to help their children remember the true God. That was a gentle answer. It stopped the war.

Let's talk: How do we usually answer when somebody yells at us? If the two tribes of Israel had answered, "Mind your own business," what might have happened? How did Jesus answer His enemies when He was hanging on the cross? How would you answer if someone said, "You're a liar"? Why is a gentle answer better than an angry answer? Memorize the Bible verse.

Older children and adults may read: 1 Peter 2:21–25

Let's pray: Dear Father in heaven, forgive us for becoming angry. Help us to be kind and gentle, like Jesus, who didn't use angry words when people made fun of Him. In His name we pray for a heart that is willing to give gentle answers. Amen.

The blood of Jesus, His Son, purifies us from all sin. 1 John 1:7

More Wonderful Than Soap

"Dad, I got some tar on my hand, and I can't wash it off," Jeffrey called from the bathroom.

"I think I know what will take it off," answered Dad. He went to the cabinet below the sink and took out a can of greasy soap. "Rub this on your hand, and then dry it off on a paper towel. Don't use any water."

Jeffrey did what his dad told him. Sure enough, his hand was clean, cleaner than it had been for a long time.

"That's great stuff!" Jeffrey said. "I bet it could clean anything."

"You might be right, but I know one place it can't clean," Dad replied. "It can't clean your heart. There's only one thing that cleans a person's heart."

"What's that?" Jeffrey asked.

"The blood of Jesus," answered Dad. "Remember the Bible verse that says, 'The blood of Jesus Christ cleans us from all sin'?"

"Why does our heart need cleaning?" Jeffrey asked. "It's inside our body, and dirt can't touch it."

"When the Bible talks about our heart, it means what we think and feel," Dad explained.

"Oh," said Jeffrey. He thought for a moment. "Sometimes I think wrong things or have bad feelings. Is that because my heart isn't clean?"

"That's right," said his dad. "Sin is like dirt or tar that won't come off with water. But when we ask God to take away our sins, then 'The blood of Jesus, His Son, purifies us from all sin.' That's because He paid for all our sins when He died on the cross."

Let's talk: What does the Bible mean when it says that everyone's heart is dirty? Is it really our heart or our thinking that is dirty? What washes away our sins and cleans our hearts? How did Jesus give His blood for the sins of all people? How does His blood wash our heart clean? Memorize the Bible verse.

Older children and adults may read: 1 John 1:5–10

Let's pray: Thank You, dear Lord Jesus, for dying for us on the cross. Forgive what we have done wrong today. We're glad that You wash away all our sins. Please keep our hearts clean by helping us not to sin. Amen.

Ears that hear and eyes that see—the Lord has made them both. Proverbs 20:12

Two Reasons for Being Happy

"I'd rather lose my eyes than my ears," said Rory. "As long as I had my ears, I could hear people talk. They could tell me everything, and I could talk back to them. I could also listen to the radio."

"I'd rather lose my ears than my eyes," said Joan. "As long as I could see people or flowers or my dog or what's around me, I'd be happy."

Rory and Joan discussed ears and eyes for a long time. Both said that it's good to have eyes and good to have ears. And those who have both have two good reasons for being thankful to God.

The Bible reminds us that "ears that hear and eyes that see—the Lord has made them both." Only the eyes that God makes can see, and only the ears that God makes can hear. People can make imitation eyes, but they can't see like a real human eye. And people can make imitation ears, but they can't hear like a real human ear.

A blind man would be very thankful if he could see. A deaf woman would be happy if she could hear. If we can hear and see, we can be doubly happy and thank God.

Let's talk: If you couldn't have both, which do you think it would be better to have, eyes or ears? Why? What's the difference between an imitation eye and the eye God makes? What kind of ear can't we make? How would people who were blind or deaf feel if they suddenly could see or hear? What reasons do we have for being thankful and happy?

Older children and adults may read: Proverbs 20:11–15

Let's pray: For our wonderful eyes we thank You, dear God. We thank You also for ears that can hear. Please forgive us if we have used our eyes and ears for sinful seeing and hearing. Help us use them only for what is good. We ask this in Jesus' name. Amen.

Honor your father and mother. Ephesians 6:2

The Captains of Our Home

"We want Richard to be our captain," said the kids on the ball team. So Richard said he would be their captain. But when he told Peter to play first base, Peter said, "Not me. I want to bat."

When Richard told Allison to play third base, Allison said, "I won't play third base. I want to be the pitcher."

Nobody wanted to do what Richard asked them to do. They said he was their captain, but they didn't honor him as their captain. Pretty soon, Richard quit trying to be the captain.

God gives parents to children. God wants parents to be the captains of their families. God has said, "Honor your father and mother." He wants children to obey their parents, love them, and help them.

How can parents do their best for their children if their children don't honor them? How can they teach their children if they won't listen? How can a home be happy if children do what they want instead of listening to their parents?

God wants children to obey their parents. But that's not the main thing. "Honor them," God says. To honor parents means to love and obey them. It means letting the parents decide how things should be, like the captain of a team. Children who honor their parents gladly do what they ask.

God also expects parents to love their children and take good care of them. He wants parents to teach their children about God so they can grow up as His children. He especially wants parents to teach their children that Jesus is their Savior. Then when children forget to honor their parents, they know they can ask God for forgiveness.

Let's talk: Why did Richard quit as the captain of the ball team? Who are the captains in our home? Who made them the captains? Why should we listen to them? What does it mean to "Honor your father and mother"? Which homes are happier—those in which the parents are honored or those in which the children try to be the captains?

Older children and adults may read: Ephesians 6:1–4

Let's pray: Dear Father in heaven, we know that we don't always honor our parents. Forgive us for Jesus' sake, and help us to do Your will. Amen.

The day is [God's], and ... also the night. Psalm 74:16

Why God Made the Night

Karen was afraid of the dark. She liked to go outside and play during the day. But when it was dark, she would not go outside unless her mother was with her. Karen was even afraid to go into her bedroom without a light.

One night Karen prayed, "Thank You, God, for the sunshine and for the daytime." But she didn't thank Him for the night.

"Why don't you thank God for the night also?" Mom asked.

"I don't like the night," Karen answered.

"Would you like to learn a special Bible verse? It tells us who makes the night," Mom said.

Karen nodded her head. Mother sat next to Karen on the bed and held her hands. "The verse is part of a psalm. It says 'The day is God's, and ... also the night.' "

Karen repeated the verse. "Does the night really belong to God? Does God make it?" she asked.

"Yes," answered Mom. "Don't you remember how God made the sun to shine by day and the moon to shine at night? God makes it dark so that people won't work all the time. Even most animals and plants rest at night. When it's dark, it's easier to sleep. God made the night so that you could sleep well."

"Maybe I'll try going to sleep without a light tonight, Mom," Karen said. So Mom turned off the night light, and soon Karen was asleep.

Let's talk: Why didn't Karen like the night? Why didn't she thank God for it? What Bible verse did her mother tell her? What is one reason God made the night dark? Why was Karen willing to go to sleep without a light?

Older children and adults may read: Psalm 74:12–17

Let's pray: Dear Father in heaven, we're glad that You give us sunshine and light, but we thank You also for the night. Give us all a quiet sleep so that we'll feel rested in the morning. We ask this in Jesus' name. Amen.

[Jesus said,] *"God is spirit."* John 4:24

What Does God Look Like?

A painter wanted to show God creating the world. He painted a big man with great big cheeks and wind blowing out of his mouth. The painting represented God sending the wind to separate the water from the land.

Another painter who wanted to paint God made a bright light coming from some clouds. He didn't show God at all. The bright light was to show that God was near.

A third painter made God look like an old man with white hair. This was supposed to be a picture of our Father in heaven.

But God is spirit. In some ways, a spirit is like a voice on the radio. You don't get a chair for that voice to sit on, do you? You don't give it something to eat. You can't see it. But the voice is really in the room with you.

When Jesus said, "God is spirit," He meant that God has no body. You can't see a spirit. But God is everywhere at all times. Of course, people saw God when Jesus lived on earth because Jesus is God. But now no one knows what God the Father in heaven looks like. We only know that He is great and powerful and kind and good.

So which painter was closest to being right? Perhaps it was the one who painted the light shining out of the clouds.

Let's talk: Can you think of something that is real even though you can't see it? Can you see the air around you or the wind? Can you draw a picture of love? Why can't we see God even though He is always with us and near us? What did Jesus mean when He said, "God is spirit"?

Older children and adults may read: John 4:19–26

Let's pray: Dear God, we're glad that You are kind and that You live in our hearts. Teach us to love You more. Make us more like Jesus by giving us the Holy Spirit to help us. We ask this in Jesus' name. Amen.

Remember the wonders [God] has done. Psalm 105:5

Wonderful Things God Can Do

Two baseball teams were playing an exciting game.

"My daddy is going to hit a home run," said Kirsten. She knew that her daddy could. How did she know? Her daddy had done it in the last game he played. That's why Kirsten believed her daddy could do it again.

Kirsten thought her daddy was the strongest man in the whole world. She remembered what her daddy could do. She was proud and happy that her daddy was so strong.

Our Father in heaven is much stronger than any father on earth. He is almighty. That means He can do anything He wants to do. He has done many wonderful things. The Bible is full of stories of wonderful things God did long ago.

While Jesus was on earth, He did many wonderful things that showed He was God. He healed sick people who came to Him. He fed 5,000 people with just five loaves of bread and two fish. He stopped a big storm on a lake. He even made dead people live again.

The Bible says, "Remember the wonders [God] has done." When we remember them, we will know that God can do wonderful things for us.

⁂

Let's talk: Why did Kirsten think her daddy could hit a home run? What are some wonderful things our Father in heaven has done? Why should we remember the wonderful things God has done? The most wonderful thing God did was sending His Son to die for us. Why did He do this?

Older children and adults may read: Psalm 105:1–5

Let's pray: You loved us so much, dear God, that You sent Jesus to save us. Please help us remember all that You have done. Then we won't be afraid the next time we're in trouble because we'll know You will help us. We praise and thank You for all Your wonderful works, especially for sending Jesus to save us. Amen.

Wash ... and cleanse me from my sins. Psalm 51:2

How God Forgives Sins

"What happens to our sins when God forgives them?" Michelle asked her mother. "Where do they go?"

"Well, where did all the marks your teacher wrote on the chalkboard yesterday go?" Mother asked.

"She just erased them, and then Terrence and I washed the chalkboard real good," Michelle answered. "All the marks are gone."

"That's what happens to our sins when God forgives them, Michelle," said Mother. "They're washed away. They're all gone."

Isn't God's forgiveness wonderful? Our angry words, our lies, all the times we disobey or treat others unkindly—where are all these sins? When we ask God to forgive us for Jesus' sake, they're washed away. They're forgiven. God says He won't even remember them.

God forgives us because Jesus paid for all sins. Jesus paid for them by dying on the cross for us. Can we ever thank Jesus enough for that? One way we thank Him is by not wanting to sin anymore.

⤚

Let's talk: Where do our sins go when they're forgiven? Who forgives them? Why is God willing to forgive our sins? In the Lord's Prayer, how do we ask for forgiveness of sins? What are some of the sins that God washes away?

Older children and adults may read: Psalm 51:1–3, 9–11

Let's pray: Dear Father in heaven, we're ashamed of our many sins, and we're sorry. Please wash us and make us clean for Jesus' sake. Amen.

Do not hate your brother in your heart. Leviticus 19:17

Don't Lose Your Temper

Seiji could get angry so easily! When some little thing did not suit him, he would stamp his feet. He would scream. He would even roll on the ground.

As Seiji grew older, he still had a bad temper. If people didn't do what he wanted, he said mean things or pouted and planned ways of hurting people to get even.

Seiji noticed that his little brother, Akeno, did not get angry easily. "Seiji, why can't you be more gentle and kind?" his mother said. "I'm glad Akeno doesn't get so angry." That made Seiji angry at his brother.

When a person is angry with someone for a long time, it's called *hate*. Long ago there were two brothers, Cain and Abel. Cain began to hate Abel. One day the two were out in a field. Cain became so angry that he killed his brother. What started as hatred turned into murder.

God tells us in the Bible, "Do not hate your brother in your heart." God wants us to love, not to hate. He wants us to be like Him. The Bible says, "God is love."

God loved the whole world very much. He sent His Son, Jesus, to die for the sins of all people—even for those who hate their brothers or kill other people. Jesus suffered and died because He loved us. Jesus said, "A new command I give you: Love one another. As I have loved you, so you must love one another. By this all men will know that you are My disciples, if you love one another."

Let's talk: Why is it a sin to hate someone? Why did Seiji often become angry? Who do you think was happier, Seiji or Akeno? What happened when Cain became angry? When we feel ourselves getting angry, what would be a good thing to do?

Older children and adults may read: Genesis 4:3–8

Let's pray: Heavenly Father, please forgive us for getting angry so easily. Keep us from losing our temper and hating those around us. Make us loving and kind, more like Jesus, every day. In His name. Amen.

[Jesus said,] "She did what she could." Mark 14:8

Doing the Best You Can

A man named Simon had invited Jesus and His disciples to his house for dinner. It was just a few days before Jesus died on the cross.

While they were eating, a woman named Mary came into the room. She was carrying a little jar of very expensive perfume. She wanted to show Jesus how much she loved Him. She stood next to Jesus and poured the perfume on His head. The smell of the perfume went all through the house.

A disciple called Judas scolded Mary. "Why has this perfume been wasted?" he asked. "It might have been sold, and the money could have been given to the poor." Some of the other disciples agreed with Judas.

Mary thought this was the best way she had to show how much she loved Jesus. When Jesus heard Judas scold Mary, He said, "Leave her alone. Why do you bother her? She has done the best thing she could."

Jesus didn't want Mary to feel ashamed of what she had done. He appreciated her gift of love.

Aren't you glad that Jesus looks at the reasons people do things? Sometimes we try to do something good, and it seems to turn out all wrong. But when Jesus knows that we have done something out of love for Him, He's pleased. He says "You have done the best you could."

Let's talk: What did Mary do for Jesus? Why did some of the guests scold her? What did Jesus say to them? Why was Jesus pleased with what Mary had done? What does Jesus think of the things we do out of love for Him?

Older children and adults may read: Mark 14:3–9

Let's pray: We're glad that You were so kind to Mary, dear Jesus, and that You look at the reasons we do things, not just what we do. Help us give You our best as a thank You for loving us. We love You, as Mary did. Amen.

Pray for those who persecute you. Matthew 5:44

What You Can Do to Get Even

Rocks were flying. People were throwing them at a man named Stephen for saying that he believed in Jesus. The rocks hit his chest; they hit his face and his back. Pretty soon he would be dead.

Just before Stephen died, he prayed. Did he ask God to punish his enemies? No! He said, "Lord, please don't punish them for this sin." When he had said that, Stephen died.

Stephen prayed for his enemies. Where had he learned to do that? He learned it from Jesus. When the soldiers were nailing Jesus to the cross, Jesus didn't hate them. Instead, He prayed for them and said, "Father, forgive them, for they don't know what they're doing."

That's the way Jesus wants us to treat people who aren't nice to us. Can you remember this Bible verse: "Love your enemies and pray for those who persecute you"? The next time you feel angry at someone, try doing what Jesus did: Pray for the person.

Let's talk: What happened to Stephen because he said he believed in Jesus? What did he do for his enemies? From who did Stephen learn this? When did Jesus pray for those who were mean to Him? Why is it hard to pray for someone we don't like? Who helps us pray for our enemies?

Older children and adults may read: Acts 7:54–60

Let's pray: Dear Jesus, we know how much You love us—enough to forgive us for the many things we do wrong. Help us forgive and pray for those who do wrong things to us. Amen.

[Jesus said,] "My words will never pass away." Matthew 24:35

Jesus Will Keep His Word

"Yes, I will build you a house," the carpenter said. But he fell from a roof and died. His words were forgotten. He didn't build the house as he had said. He couldn't keep his word.

"Yes, I will sell you a car that won't give you any trouble," said the salesman. But his words didn't come true. A few months later, the car gave the new owner a lot of trouble. The salesman's promise wasn't any good.

Many of our words pass away too. We can't keep all our promises. But Jesus said, "My words will never pass away." The words of Jesus will come true, no matter what happens.

When Jesus says, "I will forgive your sins," we can believe it. He will do it. When Jesus says, "I am with you," we can believe it. It's really true. When Jesus says, "I will give you eternal life in heaven," we can believe it.

Jesus keeps all His promises. That's what He meant when He said, "My words will never pass away." Isn't that good news?

~

Let's talk: Why couldn't the carpenter keep his promise? What happened to the salesman's promise? Whose words will never pass away? Why are we glad about that? Memorize the Bible verse.

Older children and adults may read: John 10:27–30

Let's pray: Lord Jesus, how happy we are to know that Your words will never pass away, especially Your wonderful promises. Help us keep them in our minds and hearts so that we won't forget them. Thank You for promising that You will always keep Your word. Amen.

Love comes from God. 1 John 4:7

Where Love Comes From

"Julaine is very good about taking care of Andrew. They seem to love each other very much," said Mr. Schroeder to Julaine's dad.

"God wants us to love each other, doesn't He?" Julaine said to her father after Mr. Schroeder had gone home.

"Yes, Julaine, He does," answered Dad. "I know a Bible verse that says exactly that: 'Love one another, for love comes from God.' "

Julaine repeated the verse. She wanted to remember it. She said it a few more times so she wouldn't forget it.

"All love comes from God," explained Dad. "And anybody who doesn't love, doesn't know how God thinks and feels. But those who love have God in their hearts, and they know what God is like. You know how much God loves us, don't you, Julaine?"

"Yes," Julaine said, "God showed how much He loves us by sending Jesus to die for us. My Sunday school teacher told me that."

The Bible says, "Since God so loved us, we also ought to love one another." Those who have Jesus in their hearts love one another because He is full of love.

⁀

Let's talk: How did God show His love for us? Why was Jesus willing to die for us? Why will we love other people when Jesus is in our hearts? Can Jesus stay in the hearts of those who don't love others? Why not?

Older children and adults may read: 1 John 4:7–11

Let's pray: Dear Jesus, our God and Lord, we know how full of love You are, and we're glad that You give love to the world. We wish everybody would love everyone else; how wonderful that would be! Please live in our hearts, Lord Jesus, so that we will love one another. Amen.

"He saved others … but He can't save Himself!"
Matthew 27:42

Why Jesus Died

When Jesus was hanging on the cross, the people who hated Him didn't feel sorry for Him. They made fun of Him and dared Him to come down from the cross. Even though Jesus' enemies were laughing at Him when they said it, one thing they said was true. "He saved others," they said, "but He can't save Himself."

That's exactly why Jesus stayed on the cross instead of coming down. Jesus could have saved Himself. But if He had, then He would not have saved us. To save others, Jesus couldn't save Himself. To save you and me from God's punishment for sin, Jesus had to stay on the cross and die in our place.

You can think of it another way. Once there was a great flood. A family sat on the roof of their house, waiting to be rescued. A rescue worker came by in a little boat. It had enough room for all but one. If everyone tried to get in, the boat would sink. "Save my family and leave me here," said the father. To save the others, he couldn't save himself.

There is a story about a hen that sat on her nest in some dry grass. Ten baby chicks were under her wings. The grass was burning all around her. The hen could have flown away and saved herself, but then her chicks would have burned. The hen stayed on the nest. Her feathers burned, and she died, but under her were the chicks, safe and alive. She had saved them. That's why she couldn't save herself.

The Bible says that Jesus died for us to save us. That's why His enemies told the truth when they said mockingly, "He saved others, but He can't save Himself."

Let's talk: Who made fun of Jesus as He was hanging on the cross? What did they say? In what way were their words true? In what way were their words not true? Why couldn't the father save himself? Why couldn't the hen save herself? Do we owe Jesus anything for saving us instead of Himself?

Older children and adults may read: Matthew 27:38–44

Let's pray: Thank You, dear Lord Jesus, for staying on the cross. Thank You for saving us when You could have saved Yourself. Make us willing to help others learn what You have done for them. Amen.

For God so loved the world that He gave His one and only Son. John 3:16

Does God Love Bad People?

"You aren't supposed to do that," Benjamin said to his little sister, Heather. "When you do that, you're bad, and God doesn't love bad people."

Was Benjamin right or wrong?

He was very wrong. Everybody does wrong things, but God loves us even when we aren't good. What He doesn't love are the bad things we do.

The Bible says that God loves the whole world. God loved all people so much that He gave them a present. It was the best present He could give. He gave His Son, His only Son, to the world. He did this when He sent Jesus to be everybody's Savior.

God gave His Son, Jesus, to every person who ever lived or who will live in the world. God wants all people to believe in Jesus and live with Him in heaven.

Let's talk: What did Benjamin say about God? Why was he wrong? How did God show that He loves the world? Who is included in "the world"? Who works faith in Jesus in our hearts? What does Jesus do with all sins? What does Jesus promise to all who believe in Him?

Older children and adults may read: John 3:14–17

Let's pray: Thank You, dear God, for loving the whole world and all people in it even though they sin. Please forgive us when we're bad. Help us live the way You want us to live. Thank You for sending Jesus to be our Savior and make us Your children. In His name. Amen.

Christ died for our sins. 1 Corinthians 15:3

What He Did Counts for Me

Latoya was crying softly. She was sitting on her bed in her pajamas, looking in her Bible at a picture of Jesus nailed to the cross.

"Why are you crying?" Daddy asked.

"They put nails through Jesus' hands and feet," said Latoya as she brought the book to her daddy. "He let them do it to Him because He loves us."

"Yes, Jesus loved us that much," Daddy said. "He was willing to be hurt so that we wouldn't be punished for the bad things we do."

"Like when I hit Anika?" asked Latoya. Anika was her sister.

"Yes. Or when you don't listen to your mother," Daddy answered.

Latoya climbed up on her daddy's lap and hugged him. "I love you real much, Daddy," she said. "But Jesus loved us even more, didn't He?"

"Yes, He did," said Daddy. "He did all the things God wants us to do, and then He died for us. And what He did counts for us. Because of what He did, God forgives us and calls us His children."

"And that's why we can go to heaven," said Latoya. Then she kissed her daddy good night and ran off happily to bed.

⇌

Let's talk: Why was Latoya crying? Why did Jesus let people hang Him on a cross? What do we mean when we say, "What Jesus did counts for us"? Why was Latoya happy when she went to bed? Memorize the Bible verse.

Older children and adults may read: Luke 23:44–49

Let's pray: We thank You, dear Jesus, for all that You did for us so that our sins could be forgiven. Help us never to forget how You suffered and died. Make us sorry for sinning and help us live as You want us to. Amen.

Do not give the devil a foothold. Ephesians 4:27

How to Keep from Sinning

"Don't stay in the kitchen, Kayla," said her mom. "As long as you see the cake, you'll want to taste it."

"I don't want to eat the cake. I just want to look at it," Kayla said.

"Rather than stare at the cake, let's learn a Bible verse," Mom said. "The verse says, 'Do not give the devil a foothold.' "

"Margaret says there isn't a devil," Kayla told her mom.

"Well, Jesus said there is, and He wouldn't tell us something that isn't true," Mom said. "In fact, Jesus was even tempted by the devil. The devil tries to make us do wrong, but he can't if we don't give him a chance. That's why the Bible says, 'Do not give the devil a foothold.' It means, don't let him have any place around you or in you."

Kayla thought for a minute. "When I stay near the cake, am I giving the devil a place where he can get me to do wrong?" she asked.

"I'm afraid so," said Mom.

"Then I'd better go someplace where I don't see the cake," said Kayla. "I don't want the devil to tempt me."

≈

Let's talk: Why was it wrong for Kayla to eat the cake? What Bible verse did her mother teach her? What did Kayla decide to do? Why?

Older children and adults may read: Ephesians 6:10–17

Let's pray: Dear God, we're sorry that we often give a place to the devil. Please forgive us. Help us keep the devil from having even a little place inside us. We pray in Jesus' name. Amen.

The earth is full of Your creatures. Psalm 104:24

The Riches of God

Mr. Sanders rushed into the house with an excited shout. "We're rich! Our oil well came in! It's a gusher!" he shouted to his family. "We'll never have to work again!"

The whole family piled into the car and drove to the oil field to see the well. "Don't worry, I'm going to keep on working just like before," Mr. Sanders told his wife. "Only now I'll work to help other people, not just to make money for us."

Angie and Jason watched the oil come up from beneath the ground. "It's almost as though God filled this hole with oil just for us," Angie said.

"God did fill this hole with oil for us," said Mr. Sanders.

Jason thought for a moment longer. In their geography books, the children had learned about iron and coal and diamonds and many other things hidden in the earth, ready for someone to find.

"The earth is full of good things, isn't it?" said Jason.

"That's almost a Bible verse," said Mrs. Sanders. "There's a psalm that says, 'The earth is full of [God's] creatures.' "

"Mom, there are many good things on top of the earth, too," Angie added. "There are flowers and trees and grass and bushes and hundreds of other things."

"Hey, you didn't mention animals or birds. God made them, too," Jason said.

"That's right," said Mr. Sanders, still watching the oil come out of the ground. "The earth is full of God's creatures. That's why the psalm writer said, 'I will sing to the Lord all my life; I will sing praise to my God as long as I live.' "

Let's talk: Who put the oil into the earth? What are some other good things that God put in or on the earth? Memorize the Bible verse.

Older children and adults may read: Psalm 65:9–13

Let's pray: Dear Lord, You weren't stingy when You made the earth. You made it rich with many gifts for us. We thank You for all these good things. Help us use them correctly and for the good of others, for Jesus' sake. Amen.

[Jesus said,] "Whoever does the will of My Father ... is My brother and sister and mother." Matthew 12:50

Relatives of Jesus

Who do you think came to see Jesus one day as He was teaching a large group of people? It was His mother and His brothers. Long ago cousins were also called "brothers," so maybe Jesus' "brothers" were His cousins.

These relatives of Jesus wanted to talk to Him. But the crowd was so big that they couldn't get near Him. Somebody came and told Jesus, "Your mother and Your brothers are standing back there behind all the people. They want to talk with You."

Did Jesus stop teaching and run to see His mother? No, He didn't. What He was doing was more important than talking to His mother. He was teaching the Word of God.

Jesus wanted the people to know how important the Word of God is. So He said, "Who is My mother? Who are My brothers?" Then He pointed to His disciples and said, "Look, there are My mother and My brothers. Whoever does the will of My Father is My brother and sister and mother."

How many people could be brothers and sisters and mothers of Jesus? That's right—all of us could. When we believe in Jesus and love Him, Jesus, our Savior, makes us God's children. Then we are sisters and brothers of Jesus.

Let's talk: Who came to see Jesus one day? What was Jesus doing? Why didn't He quit teaching and talk to His relatives? Who did He say were His brothers and sisters and mother? Who makes us Jesus' brothers and sisters?

Older children and adults may read: Matthew 12:46–50

Let's pray: Dear Jesus, thank You for making us children of God and Your brothers and sisters. Help us to obey our Father in heaven in all things. Amen.

It was good for me to [have trouble]. Psalm 119:71

Some Troubles Are Good

"They caught Cody stealing," Rasheeda told her mother. "I'm glad. That's good for him."

Rasheeda wasn't being nice when she said those words, but in one way, she was right. It turned out to be a good thing Cody was caught stealing.

A police officer at the station talked to Cody for a long time. "If you'll let Pastor Hiller help you, I'll give you another chance," the officer said. "Every day you have to phone or see Pastor Hiller. You need to tell him where you are and what you're doing. And you have to go to church and Sunday school."

Cody promised to do as the police officer said. Cody and Pastor Hiller became good friends. Pastor Hiller reminded Cody often that he was one of God's children.

"You belong to God," said Pastor Hiller. "Jesus suffered and died on the cross for your sins so that you could have them all forgiven. He's willing to forgive you for stealing. Because God's children love Him, they don't want to steal."

"I'm sorry I stole," Cody said. "I forgot what it means to be God's child. I'm asking Jesus to help me every day so that I won't steal anymore."

Let's talk: How did Cody get into trouble? How did God turn Cody's trouble into something good? What did Cody promise the police officer? What good came out of his trouble? What trouble have we had in our family? Did any good come out of it? Memorize the Bible verse.

Older children and adults may read: Psalm 119:71–77

Let's pray: Dear loving Lord Jesus, help us never forget that You have made us God's dear children. Teach us to live as God's children, even when we have trouble. Thank You for turning our troubles into good. Amen.

[God said,] "I live in a high and holy place, but also with him who is ... lowly in spirit. Isaiah 57:15

Two Places Where God Lives

"I wish I could be Mrs. Albern," Paulo said to Deanna.

"Why?" she asked.

"In the summer, when it's nice here, Mrs. Albern lives here. In the winter, when it's cold here, she lives in Florida," Paulo explained. "She has two places to live."

"I know somebody else who lives in two places," said Deanna.

"Who?" asked Paulo.

"God. He lives up in heaven, and He lives in my heart," she answered.

"He does?" asked Paulo with a confused look. "How do you know that?"

"My mother read that in the Bible and told me," Deanna replied. Deanna ran inside to ask her mother to bring her Bible and show the verse to Paulo.

"Let me read what God says in the Bible," Deanna's mother said. " 'I live in a high and holy place, but also with him who is ... lowly in spirit.' "

"The high and holy place is heaven, isn't it?" asked Deanna.

"Yes," said her mother, "and the people who have lowly spirits are those who know they aren't good enough to live with God," Mother added. "They know they need His forgiveness."

"Will God live in my heart too?" Paulo asked.

"Certainly! God will be glad to live with you," Deanna's mother said with a smile. "He will forgive your sins for Jesus' sake, and make you His child."

Let's talk: God is everywhere, but in which two places does this Bible verse say God lives? Where is the high and holy place? What kind of people have lowly spirits? Why does God live in our hearts? Memorize the Bible verse.

Older children and adults may read: Isaiah 57:19–21

Let's pray: Dear Lord, we know that we aren't holy like You. We know that on our own, we aren't good enough to have You live with us. But we thank You for sending Jesus to take away our sin. Now You can live with us. Forgive our sins and keep us as Your dear children, for Jesus' sake. Amen.

[God says,] "I am the first, and I am the last; apart from Me there is no God." Isaiah 44:6

Make-Believe Gods

Dawn wanted a little sister. But God didn't give her a little sister. So Dawn put some dresses on her biggest doll and said, "This is my sister, Brittany." But she was pretending. Only God can make a sister. Nobody can make a sister out of a doll.

Many years before Jesus lived on earth, the people of Israel loved the Lord God and were His children. But people in the countries around Israel made their own gods. They made a person or an animal out of a stone or a tree and called these statues their gods.

These gods were pretend gods. But the people thought they were real. They even prayed to them. Dawn knew better than that. She couldn't make a real sister, so how could anyone make a real god?

Today many people still make their own gods. In India and Africa and Japan and even in the United States, children pray to gods who really aren't gods. Sometimes people don't pray to a person or an animal, but they love something more than God. What are some things people love? Money, houses, cars, television, candy, and many other things. We make these things our gods if we love them more than we love the real God.

Do we love God more than anything else? He is the one real God who loves us. That's why He is first and last and most important in our hearts.

⌒

Let's talk: How did Dawn make a sister? What are some things people might love more than God? Who is the only real God who ever was or ever will be? Who should be most important in our lives?

Older children and adults may read: Isaiah 44:1–6

Let's pray: We are glad, dear God, that You are our God and that You always will be. We want nobody else but You for our God. Forgive us for not always loving You more than anything else. Help us trust in You above all things. In Jesus' name. Amen.

Create in me a pure heart, O God. Psalm 51:10

How to Get Clean on the Inside

King David was feeling very bad. He had sinned. He had taken the pretty wife of one of his soldiers. Then he had gotten rid of the soldier by putting him in the front of a battle. There the soldier was killed, as David had hoped.

For a while David pretended that he hadn't done anything wrong. He wouldn't even tell God he was sorry.

But God sent the prophet Nathan to David. "God has been very good to you. Why have you done this great sin?" Nathan asked. "You killed Uriah and have taken his wife to be your wife. A lot of trouble will come to you now. Because God's enemies are making fun of what you have done, your child will die."

Now David knew that God had seen what he had done, and he was very upset. "I have sinned against God," David cried. What could he do?

David asked God to take his sins away. "Please feel sorry for me, dear God," he said. Then the Holy Spirit helped David write a poem others still use to ask God for forgiveness. It's Psalm 51 in the Bible.

In Psalm 51, King David begged God to forgive his sins. "Create in me a pure heart, O God," he said. He knew that only God could wash away the wrong he had done. For seven days and nights the king prayed. He wouldn't even eat.

King David was punished, as Nathan said he would be. But because he begged God to wash his sins away, God forgave David.

"Create in me a pure heart, O God." That's a prayer everyone needs to say because so often we think and say and do what isn't right. Every sin is like dirt in our hearts, and only God can make our hearts clean. He does this when He forgives all our sins for Jesus' sake.

Let's talk: What sin did King David do? What did the prophet Nathan tell him? Which psalm, or poem, did King David write after Nathan talked to him? What did David beg for in this psalm? What does "create" mean? How does God make our hearts pure and clean?

Older children and adults may read: Psalm 51:10–12

Let's pray: Create in me a pure heart, O God, by washing away all my sins for Jesus' sake. Amen.

Do not let the sun go down while you are still angry.
Ephesians 4:26

Smile before Sundown

Stephen and Troy were working in a factory. Stephen bent down to pick up a hammer. When he straightened up, he hit the back of his head on a board. Troy laughed. That made Stephen very angry. Without thinking, he hit Troy with the hammer. Troy died. Stephen had killed his best friend.

Not all anger is wrong. God gets angry at sin.

Remember how angry Jesus was when He chased the money changers out of the temple? We need to be angry about sin. God wants us to get rid of sin in our lives.

But anger is a difficult emotion to control. It's so easy to get angry at people and to get angry without a good reason. When we get so angry that we want to hurt people, we don't love them. God wants us to love even our worst enemies.

Many people can't stop being angry with others. In our Bible verse, Paul tells us we shouldn't let the sun go down on our anger. This means, if we do become angry about something, we should ask God to help us solve the problem before the end of the day. Anger that keeps on burning inside of us turns into hate, and hate is even more dangerous than anger.

Remember Cain and Abel? Cain was jealous and angry because God was more pleased with Abel than with him. Cain let his anger grow day after day, and soon it turned into hate.

Ask Jesus to help you forgive and forget so that the sun won't go down on your anger. Jesus will help you follow His example and love everyone—even your enemies.

⁓

Let's talk: What did Stephen do to Troy? Why did he do it? Why is anger so dangerous? Why shouldn't we get angry at people? If we are angry day after day, what does our anger become? What does Paul say in the Bible verse?

Older children and adults may read: Matthew 6:12–15

Let's pray: Our Father in heaven, You are very patient and slow to get angry. Help us to be like You. Make us kind and gentle, like Jesus, and teach us to become angry only at sin. When we become angry with people, help us get over it before the sun goes down. We ask this in Jesus' name. Amen.

[Jesus said,] "I am with you always." Matthew 28:20

We Are Never Alone

Juanita was crying. The older children had gone to the river to swim, but Juanita was too young to go along—she had to stay home. That's why she was crying.

"I'm all alone," Juanita told her mom. "Nobody's here to play with me."

"Why don't you come and help me bake a cake?" asked Mom.

Juanita wiped her tears and went into the kitchen. Mom helped her measure out the flour and mix it with milk and butter and sugar and other ingredients. It was fun to help Mom. Soon a big smile spread across Juanita's face.

"I'm not alone now," she said, "not when I'm with you, Mom."

God's children are never alone. God is always with them. And God is always everywhere. Sometimes we feel all alone and sad or sick and worried. Sometimes we think that nobody loves us, and then we feel horribly alone. But we're never alone. Jesus said, "I am with you always."

Let's talk: Why was Juanita crying? Who made Juanita smile? How? Why are we never alone? Why do we sometimes feel sad and lonely? To whom can we speak when we feel alone? In how many places is Jesus at the same time?

Older children and adults may read: John 16:28–33

Let's pray: Dear Lord Jesus, we're glad that You are always with us, even when nobody else is near. Help us remember that You are always with us, that You love us and are always ready to help us. Please forgive our sins and remind us always of Your love for us. Amen.

[Jesus said,] "Learn from Me, for I am gentle and humble in heart. Matthew 11:29

Our Lord Is Never Proud

Some soldiers were building a fort. They were having a hard time lifting a log into place. "Heave away! Heave ho!" shouted the corporal. He shouted at his men, but he did not help them.

A man on horseback rode up, stopped, jumped off his horse, and helped the soldiers. Then he turned to the corporal and said, "Why didn't you help them?"

"Me?" asked the corporal. "I'm an officer!" He was too proud to help the common soldiers work. He was too proud to help his men.

Do you know what the rider said as he swung up onto his horse? "The next time you need help on work you're too proud to do, call George Washington." The corporal almost fainted. Now he knew the man who helped was the general in charge of all the soldiers.

Do you think Jesus would have helped the men? Or would He have been too proud to help, like the corporal? Jesus wasn't too proud to do anything that needed to be done to help *us*. He wasn't too proud to help His parents. He wasn't too proud to go to school. He wasn't too proud to work.

Jesus was not ashamed to have poor people as His friends, not even when other people called them sinners. He loves all of us even though He is great and we are nothing. Even though Jesus is God, He wasn't too proud to suffer and die for us.

That's something we can learn from Jesus. "Learn from Me," He said, "for I am gentle and humble in heart." To be humble means you don't think you're better than anyone else. Jesus helps us learn to be humble.

Let's talk: Who was too proud to help his soldiers? Who was humble enough to help the soldiers? How did Jesus show that He isn't proud? What does Jesus say in our Bible verse? How can we learn to be humble?

Older children and adults may read: Matthew 11:28–30

Let's pray: Dear Jesus, we're glad that You weren't too proud to be a baby and a man to save us. Thank You for being willing to die for us on the cross. Teach us how to be humble in heart as You are. Amen.

[Jesus prayed,] "Father ... *not My will, but Yours be done.*
Luke 22:42

Doing What God Wants

Twelve men walked down a hill. They went over a creek and up another hill to a garden park. One of the men, the group's leader, was very sad. He was thinking of something that was about to happen.

Soon the group came to the park gate. There the leader said to eight of the men, "Stay here and wait for Me; I want to go into the park and pray for awhile."

The leader took three of His best friends with Him. They walked farther into the garden. The leader asked the three to wait there and pray while He went to pray by Himself. The three men sat down. The leader went away about as far as you can throw a stone. He kneeled down and talked to His Father in heaven.

"My Father," He prayed, "please don't let Me suffer and die. But if I must do this to save all people, then I will. Help Me do what You want, not what I want."

Then the leader went back to His friends. His friends were sleeping. So He went away again to pray. Three times the leader did this. He knew that soon He would have to suffer and die to pay for our sins. Each time the leader said He would do what His Father in heaven wanted to be done.

That leader was Jesus. Even though He was God's Son, He could feel sorrow and pain. He didn't like hanging on the cross. But because His Father wanted Him to save us, Jesus was willing to suffer and die for us. He loved us that much.

We're thankful that Jesus suffered and died in our place. We're even more thankful that He came back to life. Because of Jesus, we have forgiveness of sins and eternal life with Him in heaven.

Let's talk: Where did Jesus go with His friends one night? Why was He sad? How often did He pray in the garden? What did He say to His Father in heaven? Why was Jesus willing to suffer and die? How can we show our love and thanks to Jesus?

Older children and adults may read: Luke 22:39–46

Let's pray: Dear Father in heaven, we know that You love us because You sent Your only Son to die for us. And Jesus loved us enough to follow Your plan. Please help us in all our troubles. But we ask that You do what You know is best for us, not what we want. In Jesus' name we pray. Amen.

Put off [lying] and speak truthfully. Ephesians 4:25

Always Tell the Truth

"Nola stole some money, I think," said Kirk.

"She did?" asked Mrs. Olandra. "Then I probably shouldn't let her run errands for me anymore. I think I should tell Mr. Samson, too. He was going to give Nola a job in his store."

Kirk felt sorry he had told Mrs. Olandra about Nola. He knew it might not be true. He wanted to tell Mrs. Olandra that he wasn't sure Nola had stolen the money, but Mrs. Olandra hurried inside her house and closed the door.

Through the window, Kirk could see Mrs. Olandra talking on the phone. She was probably telling Mr. Samson what she had heard about Nola.

By telling a lie, Kirk had probably cost Nola two jobs! He'd also spoiled the good thoughts people had about Nola. That's how much harm one little lie can do.

Lies hurt the people who tell them, the people who hear them, and the people about whom they are told. They make people think wrong things. We should even be careful about lying for fun. Sometimes these lies can hurt our friends and cause a lot of problems.

You lie when you aren't completely honest with people or when you try on purpose to make people believe what isn't true. God says, "Put off lying and speak truthfully." Liars don't follow Jesus' example of always telling the truth. They don't treat others as they want to be treated.

Let's talk: What did Kirk say about Nola? What harm did it do? What could Kirk have done? Why is it risky to say what isn't true, even if you're just having fun? What is a lie? Why doesn't God want us to tell lies?

Let's pray: Dear God, we know that You hate lies. Forgive us for the lies we have told. Help us put away lying, for Jesus' sake. Amen.

[God says,] "Call upon Me in the day of trouble." Psalm 50:15

They Didn't Think God Would

King Herod put Simon Peter in jail for preaching about Jesus. The king was going to kill Peter. But the Christians in Jerusalem asked God to save Peter. The night before Peter was to be killed, God sent an angel to help him. The angel opened the door of the jail and let Peter out.

Peter went to the house where the Christians were praying. A girl named Rhoda told them that Peter was knocking at the door. "You must be crazy," they said. They didn't believe that God really answered their prayers. But Peter kept on knocking. When they finally opened the door, they were surprised to see Peter.

God promises to help us, too, when we pray to Him. "Call upon Me in the day of trouble," He says, "and I will deliver you." He loves us, and He wants to help us. He asks us to tell our troubles to Him.

Sometimes when we ask God for help, we don't really believe He can help us. But God can do anything He wants, and He will help us in any kind of trouble. So call upon God when you have trouble, and trust His promise to help you. He will.

Let's talk: Why was Peter in jail? Why were the Christians in Jerusalem praying for him? Did they expect God to answer their prayers? How can we tell? Can you remember a time when God answered your prayer? Why don't we always believe that God will answer our prayers? Memorize the Bible verse.

Older children and adults may read: Acts 12:11–17

Let's pray: Dear Lord God, we thank You for asking us to tell You all our troubles. Thank You for answering our prayers even though we don't always believe You will. Help us trust that You will always answer our prayers as You have promised. We ask this in Jesus' name. Amen.

There will be no more … crying. Revelation 21:4

What Heaven Is Like

Sergei had an operation on his eyes. His family waited for the doctor to take off the bandages. "Either he will see well, or he won't see at all," the doctor explained as he began removing the bandages.

Layer after layer of bandages came off. After the last one, Sergei put his hands in front of his eyes. "I can't see," he said slowly. "I must be blind."

His mother started to cry. "Don't cry, Mom," Sergei said quietly. "I can wait until Jesus takes me to heaven. In heaven I'll see again."

What a wonderful thing to know. There'll be no problems in heaven. Nobody will be blind. Nobody will be crying. There will be nothing to cry about when we're in heaven.

Heaven is where Jesus wants us all to be. That's why He came to save us. That's why He died for us on the cross. That's why He rose again on the first Easter. Aren't you glad He did this for all of us?

Let's talk: What do you think most children would say if they found out they were blind? How did knowing about heaven help Sergei? Who do you think told Sergei about heaven? What things do people cry about? Will these things be in heaven? How do we get to heaven?

Older children and adults may read: Revelation 21:1–4

Let's pray: Thank You, dear God, for promising that Your children will be with You in heaven someday. We ask for Your help in all our troubles. Keep us close to You for Jesus' sake. Amen.

In the beginning God created the heavens and the earth.
Genesis 1:1

God Made Everything

Akima and her mother took her baby sister out for a walk. They stopped to rest under a big tree.

"Who made this tree, Mother?" Akima asked.

"Akima, you know who made this tree," said Mother.

Akima laughed. "I was just having some fun," she said. "I know that God made this tree. He made all the trees in all the parks and on all the farms and in all the woods and …" Akima was almost out of breath.

"Not only the trees but also the bushes and the flowers and the corn and the wheat," added Mother.

"And the water and the clouds and the stars and the sun and everything—the whole world," Akima continued, waving both arms in a big circle.

"Mother, when was 'in the beginning'?" Akima asked.

"The beginning was when God created the heavens and the earth," answered Mother. "God didn't have any beginning. But one day He started creating the heavens and the whole earth, and that was 'in the beginning.'"

Akima was quiet for the longest time. She was thinking of how God had created so many things, including big stars and tiny little bugs. She remembered how He had created them just by saying, "Let there be."

Let's talk: When did God create the first trees? What do flowers tell us about God? What did God use to create the world? Who alone can create something out of nothing?

Older children and adults may read: Genesis 1:11–28

Let's pray: Dear almighty Father, Maker of heaven and earth, how great, how wise, how good You are! Thank You for creating all things beautiful. Help us be the kind of people You want us to be. We ask this in the name of Jesus, our Savior. Amen.

[Jesus] loved me and gave Himself for me. Galatians 2:20

Why Jesus Gave His Life Away

A boat turned over on a lake. The boy who had been fishing in it sank under the water. A man on the shore saw what happened and swam to where the boy had gone under. The man rescued the boy. Then he wrapped the boy in a blanket and took him home to a very happy family.

But the man who saved the boy caught a bad cold. He became so sick, he died.

The boy never forgot the man who saved him. His parents also were thankful. They helped the man's family. Every year the boy went to the cemetery and put flowers on the man's grave. He said, "That man saved me and died for me."

Those words sound almost like the words the apostle Paul used about Jesus. He said, "Jesus loved me and gave Himself for me." But Jesus loved all of us much more than anyone else could love us. He lived a humble life on earth even though He was God. And He let people hurt Him and nail Him to the cross.

Jesus loved us and gave Himself for us. He gave His life so that we could be saved from our sins. He rose again so we could be in heaven with Him when we die. We don't want to forget Jesus. Those who believe that Jesus died for them thank Him, and tell others about Him.

Let's talk: What happened to the boy in the boat? What did the man on the shore do? Why did he die? Why were the boy and his parents thankful? How did Jesus give Himself for us? How can we show our love for Jesus?

Older children and adults may read: Galatians 2:20

Let's pray: Dear Jesus, our Savior, we never want to forget You or all the things You have done for us. Help us show You every day how thankful we are that You gave Your life for us. Amen.

[God's] years will never end. Psalm 102:27

How Old Is God?

"How old is God?" Brianna asked her teacher.

"Suppose there were a big mountain of grain a mile high," Mr. Eck said. "Suppose that every thousand years a bird came along and picked one grain off that mountain. When that mountain of grain would be eaten up, then not even one minute of God's life would be gone."

"Wow, He's pretty old!" Brianna gasped.

God has never had a birthday, so we really don't know how old He is. In fact, God never started. He just always was. He created the world. He created the sun, moon, and stars and everything that's in the whole universe. He made us. We're not very old. But God was around a long time before us. God always was. He had no beginning.

Jesus didn't have a beginning either. He's God's Son and is also God like His Father. Jesus did have an earthly life that could be measured in years. He came as a baby just like you. He grew up to become a man, just like your dad. But Jesus was God long, long before He came to earth. He had no beginning.

And God won't stop living. "God's years will never end," says the Bible. God is always the same. He never gets old and dies.

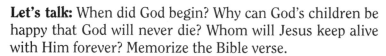

Let's talk: When did God begin? Why can God's children be happy that God will never die? Whom will Jesus keep alive with Him forever? Memorize the Bible verse.

Older children and adults may read: Psalm 102:25–28

Let's pray: Dear Jesus, we're glad that Your years will never end and that You will always be our God. Be with us every day while we live here on earth, and take us to be with You forever in heaven. Amen.

[Jesus said,] *"My Father will give you whatever you ask in My name."* John 16:23

Why We Pray in Jesus' Name

"Mom, why do we end our prayers 'in Jesus' name'? What does that mean?" Mario asked.

"To answer your question, let me tell you a story," Mom said. "It may help you understand what it means to do something in somebody else's name."

A young man named José had a beautiful horse. His country went to war and José joined the army. While fighting in a battle, José was hit by a bullet and badly wounded. His friend Roberto crept out to him and pulled him to a safe place.

José knew he was dying, so he wrote on a scrap of paper, "I want my father and mother to have everything I own, but I want Roberto to have my horse." José signed his name and gave the paper to Roberto. Then José died.

After a while, Roberto was sent home. As soon as he could, Roberto went to see José's parents. After dinner, Roberto asked for the horse. "I'm sorry. You can't have it," José's father said. "We want José's brother to have it."

Roberto showed José's father the paper. The father saw his son's name. When he read what his son wanted, he gladly gave Roberto the horse.

"I get it," Mario said. "When Roberto asked in his own name, he didn't get the horse. But when he used José's name, the father knew it was all right to give him the horse. It was what his son wanted him to do."

Mario thought for a moment. "So when we ask God for anything in our own name, we might not get it. But when we ask for things *Jesus* wants us to have God will do it."

"Yes. Jesus said, 'My Father will give you whatever you ask in My name.' Isn't that exciting?" Mother asked.

⤙

Let's talk: Why didn't Roberto get the horse at first? What made José's father willing to give Roberto the horse? Who told us to pray in Jesus' name? What does it mean to pray in Jesus' name?

Older children and adults may read: John 16:22–27

Let's pray: Dear Lord Jesus, how wonderful it is that we may ask our heavenly Father for anything in Your name. Teach us to ask for the things You want us to have. In Your name we pray. Amen.

Direct me in the path of Your commands. Psalm 119:35

Choosing the Right Path

"Be sure to stay with your leader," Mom said to Aaron. He and some other children were going on a hike in the mountains.

"I will," Aaron promised.

When they came to the first side road, the leader stopped and talked to the children. "You will see many paths along the trail," the leader explained. "Some lead to the river. Some go over the mountain. Some lead to the caves. You need to stay on the right path or you may get lost, and we won't be able to find you. Be sure to stay on the trails on which I lead you."

The children promised to follow the leader. Everyone got home safely.

God is like a guide or leader. The path on which He wants us to go is the path of His commands. His commands lead us and guide us along the paths we are to follow. God's ways are safe and good. When we don't follow God's commands, we get lost.

Because we've been saved by Jesus, we gladly follow Him. We know that He will lead us only on the right paths. He will bring us safely to our home in heaven. That's why we say, "Direct us in the path of Your commands."

Let's talk: What did the leader tell the children? Why was it important for them to stay on the right path? What if a child had said, "I'll go my own way; I know as much as the leader"? On what path does God want us to go? Why do God's children want to go on the path of God's commands?

Older children and adults may read: Psalm 119:33–36

Let's pray: Dear Father in heaven, help us follow the path of Your commands. We want to follow Jesus, our Lord and Savior. We're glad that He saved us from getting lost on the wrong paths. Keep us on the right path with Him. In His name we pray. Amen.

It is [God] who made us. Psalm 100:3

Our Maker

Paula and her father were in a hardware store. A man was talking loudly with some other people. He said, "God didn't make me. I don't even believe there is a God. We got here by ourselves."

The others didn't agree with the man. "I don't think a broom handle gets on a broom by itself," a woman said. "How could your arm get on your shoulder by itself, or how could your two eyes be just in the right place, or how could your mind work the way it does if somebody hadn't planned it?"

Paula and her father said nothing. On the way home, Paula asked, "Daddy, that man in the hardware store, he doesn't believe in God does he?"

"No, I don't think he does," Dad answered. "If he did, he would be thanking God for the way he's made instead of saying that he just grew by himself."

"That man's like the gingerbread boy who ran away and thought he could do anything by himself," said Paula.

"That's right, Paula," said Dad. "God gave that man his mind for thinking and his tongue for talking, but he used his tongue to say that there is no God."

"I'm going to thank God for making me. He sure made me wonderful," said Paula.

"I'm glad you're thankful, Paula. So am I. 'It is [God] who made us.' That's what the psalmist wrote in the Bible," Dad said.

Let's talk: What did the man in the hardware store say? What did Paula ask about the man? Why does our arm have a hand and not an ear? Why isn't our nose at the bottom of our foot? How else can we tell that God made us? How can we show God our thankfulness for our wonderful body? Memorize the Bible verse.

Older children and adults may read: Psalm 100

Let's pray: Dear Lord, we thank You for giving us eyes and ears, hands and feet, and a wonderful body that can do so many things. We thank You especially for giving us a mind that can think. Forgive us for not always using our minds well. Keep us as Your children, for Jesus' sake. Amen.

[Forgive] each other. Ephesians 4:32

How to Forgive Others

"I never want to see Chad again," cried Lioba. "He really hurt me bad."

"What did he do?" Mother asked.

"He told a lie about me. He said I never wash and never take a bath," Lioba said, crying harder. "And when we walked home, he hit a mud puddle with a stick and splashed mud all over my dress."

"But God wants us to forgive each other," said Mother. "Don't you want to forgive Chad, too?"

Lioba looked down, stamped her foot, and said, "No! The next time I see him, I'll stick out my tongue at him. And the next time he asks me to help him in school, I'll tell him to go splash some mud on himself."

Lioba's mother sighed and said, "If you can't forgive Chad, I wonder why God told us to forgive each other?"

Lioba hung her head, a little ashamed.

"God forgives us many things every day, Lioba," said

Mother. "But God also says we should forgive others because He has forgiven us. What if we said the Lord's Prayer together? Jesus will help you forgive Chad as He has forgiven you."

Mother and Lioba prayed the Lord's Prayer. When they came to the part that says, "Forgive us our trespasses, as we forgive ..." Mother stopped. "How do we want God to forgive us?" she asked.

"As we forgive ..." began Lioba. "As I forgive Chad," she whispered.

After a while, Lioba told her mother, "I'll forgive Chad because Jesus forgave me." Then she felt better

Let's talk: Why didn't Lioba want to forgive Chad? What did her mother ask? When we pray the Lord's Prayer, how do we ask God to forgive us? Who made Lioba willing to forgive Chad? Memorize the Bible verse.

Older children and adults may read: Ephesians 4:30–32

Let's pray: Dear Father in heaven, You forgive all the sins we do for Jesus' sake. Help us forgive the sins people do against us, as You forgive us. In His name. Amen.

Trust in the Lord and do good. Psalm 37:3

God's Children Trust in Jesus

Linda was just learning to read. She read a Bible verse in her Sunday school lesson. It said, "Trust in the Lord and do good."

"Mother, what does 'trust' mean?" Linda asked.

Her mother lifted Linda up on the kitchen table. Then she stepped back and spread her arms. "Jump, Linda," Mother said, just the way she used to when Linda was smaller. Linda smiled and jumped.

"How did you know I wouldn't let you fall?" Mother asked.

"Oh, I just knew," answered Linda. "You'd never let me get hurt."

"You trust me, Linda. You jumped because you trusted me. If you had been afraid that I wouldn't catch you, you wouldn't have jumped," Mother said.

"So I trust in the Lord when I think He'll take care of me?" asked Linda.

"Yes," said Mother. "When you trust in God, you believe that He loves you and will take care of you. But don't forget the last part of the Bible verse," said Mother. "What else does it say God's children do?"

Linda read the verse again. "I know," she said. "Because God takes care of me, I should do what God wants me to do."

"That's right. And people who know how much the Lord Jesus loves them trust that He will help them do what is right," Mother said.

≈

Let's talk: How did Linda's mother show her what *trust* means? What does *trust* mean? What can we be sure Jesus will do for us? How can we show that we trust the Lord?

Older children and adults may read: Psalm 37:1–5

Let's pray: Like a child trusts her mother, so will we trust You, dear Jesus, because You love us more than any mother ever loved her child. Please help us show our trust in You by doing what is good. Amen.

[Jesus said,] "Where two or three come together in My name, there am I with them. Matthew 18:20

The Meetings Jesus Attends

"Mother, I *have* to go to that meeting at school. Bill Cosby will be there," said Marcus. He thought nobody was as funny as Bill Cosby.

So Marcus' mother said he could go.

The next Sunday morning Marcus asked, "Do I have to go to Sunday school and church?"

"Yes, Bill Cosby may be there," Mother answered.

"Will he really?" asked Marcus.

"Would you go if he were?" she said.

"Yeah," Marcus answered.

"Well, Bill Cosby won't be there, but there'll be somebody more important," Mother said.

"More important? Who?" Marcus asked with a puzzled look on his face.

"Jesus will be there," Mother told him. "Jesus said, 'Where two or three come together in My name, there am I with them.' "

Does Jesus go to your church and Sunday school? He certainly does. The people who meet together at your church are Christians. They meet together as Jesus' followers. Jesus said, "Where two or three come together in My name, there am I with them." You don't want to miss seeing and hearing Jesus, do you?

⁂

Let's talk: Why did Marcus want to go to a meeting? Who did he think was the funniest person in the world? What great person is at our Sunday school and church every Sunday? Why do we want to go to Sunday school and church? Memorize the Bible verse.

Older children and adults may read: John 20:18–20

Let's pray: Lord Jesus, help us remember that whenever two or three or more of Your friends meet together, You are there with them. Help us to ask our friends who don't know about You to come to church and Sunday school with us. In Your name. Amen.

Has God forgotten to be merciful? Psalm 77:9

Will God Ever Forget Us?

First Mrs. McGruder's son became sick and died. Then her husband lost his job. Then somebody hit their car and smashed it.

Mrs. McGruder sat in her house and cried. "Has God stopped loving us?" she asked out loud.

No, God never stops loving anyone. We don't always know why God lets certain things happen to us. But God does have a plan for our lives, and nothing happens to us that He doesn't know about. God never stops being kind and good to us.

John Bunyan was put in jail for preaching about Jesus. While he was in jail, he wrote a book that taught many people about Jesus. Jail wasn't a good thing, but God had a good reason for letting John Bunyan be arrested.

Joseph's brothers sold him as a slave to some men traveling to Egypt. Joseph became a powerful ruler in Egypt. Later he saved many people, including his brothers, from dying when they had no food.

The writer of Psalm 77 was in great trouble. He prayed to God, but it seemed as though God didn't care. "Has God forgotten to be merciful?" he asked.

Then the writer remembered what God had done. "I will remember the deeds of the Lord," he said.

Anyone who remembers that Jesus died on the cross knows that God would never stop loving anybody. So if you ever wonder whether God has stopped loving you, think of what He has done for you.

Let's talk: Why was Mrs. McGruder crying? What did John Bunyan do while he was in jail? How did God bless Joseph in Egypt? What did Joseph eventually do? Why can we be sure that God will never stop loving us?

Older children and adults may read: Psalm 77:7–15

Let's pray: Dear God, don't let us ever think that You don't love us anymore. Help us remember at all times how You saved us and made us Your children. We're glad that You keep on loving us for Jesus' sake. Amen.

The Lord watches over you. Psalm 121:5

God Watches over Us

Jaleesa was a good babysitter. She took very good care of the children she watched. "I never worry when Jaleesa watches my children," Mr. Whitener told Jaleesa's mother. "I know I can trust her."

Jaleesa made sure the children didn't play too close to the fireplace. She played with them to keep them from arguing with each other. She told them Bible stories and taught them about Jesus. The children loved Jaleesa because she loved them.

Do you know that somebody is watching over us all the time? The Bible says, "The Lord watches over you." God isn't a babysitter, but in some ways, Jaleesa was like Him. God sees to it that we don't get hurt. He keeps us from sinning. He feeds us and gives us rest. He teaches us in the Bible and leads us to love Jesus.

"The Lord watches over you," the psalm verse says. We're always safe when we're in God's care. We can trust Him more than the very best babysitter.

Let's talk: Why did Mr. Whitener like Jaleesa? Why did the children love her? In what ways was Jaleesa a little like God? What does our Bible verse say about the Lord? In what ways is God better than any baby-sitter could be?

Older children and adults may read: Psalm 121

Let's pray: Dear God, we thank You for keeping watch over us and for loving us. We know that we often do wrong things. Forgive our sins and keep on loving us even though we don't deserve it. We ask this for Jesus' sake. Amen.

Honor the Lord ... with the firstfruits ... then your barns will be filled to overflowing. Proverbs 3:9–10

Thinking of God First

Mr. Fernando got his paycheck. "You know, after I paid my credit card bill, the electric bill, made my car payment, and bought some groceries, there wasn't much left for church!" he told some friends.

Mr. Fernando didn't remember how much the Lord loved him. He put the Lord in the wrong place. He put the Lord last. God wants the firstfruits, the very first part, of what we receive. And God promises that when we give Him the very first part, He will make sure we have everything we need.

In the Old Testament, God told His people to give their firstfruits to Him. The first ripe grain was to be the Lord's, and the first figs and the first calf and the first lambs. Does God need figs and calves and lambs? No, but God wants us to think of Him first, and He wants us to love Him more than anything else. The First Commandment says, "You will have no other gods before Me."

A man once brought the prophet Elisha 20 small loaves of bread for 100 students. It wasn't enough for so many, but God blessed it and made it enough. Those 20 loaves were his firstfruits, the man said. He gave to God before anyone else.

God promises to give us much more than we can ever give to Him when we think of Him first. After all, everything we have comes from God. We can trust His promise to provide for all our needs.

~

Let's talk: Why didn't Mr. Fernando have money for his church? What could he have done instead? What fruits did God say He wants? Why does God want to be first? What does He promise those who give Him their firstfruits? How can we give God the first part of the money we get?

Older children and adults may read: 2 Kings 4:42–44

Let's pray: Dear Lord, we don't want to love our money or anything we have as much as we love You. Forgive us for being selfish with so much of what You give us. Help us remember that we should give You the first part as a thank You for the blessings You give us. We ask this in the name of Jesus, our Savior. Amen.

[Jesus said,] "I am the Light of the world." John 9:5

Jesus Wants to Shine in Us

Everybody who came to church one evening got a candle. After the sermon, the lights were turned off. The pastor lit his candle. "Will the ushers please light their candles from mine?" he asked. They did.

As the ushers went back down the aisle, they lit the candles of the people sitting at the end of each bench. These people lit the candles of those sitting next to them and so on. Soon the whole church was bright with candlelight. It all started from one candle.

The pastor told the people what it meant. "The whole world is like a dark place," he said. "People are lost and can't see the way to heaven. People are also afraid in the dark and often do wrong things.

"But Jesus is like a bright light that is always burning," the pastor continued. "When we believe He is our Savior, He begins to shine in us.

"When Jesus shines in us, we become lights, too. We get our light from Him," the pastor said. "Then we can help light up the darkness around us. We can show people the way to heaven. We can tell them that Jesus is their Savior. We can show them the way Jesus wants us to live."

Are you a light in the world? You are—because Jesus lives in you. He shines in your heart. And when others see that you love Him, they may come to love Him, too.

≈

Let's talk: Where did the candles in the church get their light? How do lights help people? Why do we say that people who don't believe in Jesus are lost in the dark? How is Jesus like a light? Memorize the Bible verse.

Older children and adults may read: John 9:1–7

Let's pray: Dear Jesus, many people around us don't know You. They can't see that You are their Savior, and they don't love You. Please shine in our hearts so that we can help show others how wonderful You are. Amen.

With the Lord is unfailing love. Psalm 130:7

Jesus Loves Us

"Mercy sakes!" said Holly. She had heard the lady next door say that. "Mommy, what does 'mercy' mean?" she asked.

"Mercy, means love," Mommy told her. "It means someone feels sorry about something that happened to you and then tries to help you."

"Like when I fell out of the tree and that man carried me home?" Holly asked.

"Yes," said Mommy. "He showed mercy. But the person who shows us the most mercy is the Lord Jesus."

"Why does Jesus feel sorry for us?" asked Holly.

"Because without His help we're in trouble," answered Mommy.

"What kind of trouble?" Holly asked.

"Well, we haven't always done what God wants us to do, have we?" Mommy asked.

"No," answered Holly, "not always."

"But God can't let our sins go without punishment," Mommy said. "Jesus saved us from being punished by letting His Father punish Him instead of us."

Holly's mom was right. Jesus felt sorry—He had mercy—for us because we were all in trouble with God. Jesus loved us so much that He died on the cross so that everyone could have forgiveness. "With the Lord is unfailing love." That is why we love Him so much.

Let's talk: What do you think the word "mercy" means? Why did the Lord Jesus feel sorry for all people? How did He help us out of the trouble of sin? What does God give us instead of punishment? Why does God forgive us? Memorize the Bible verse.

Older children and adults may read: Psalm 130

Let's pray: Dear Lord, heavenly Father, we know that we sin every day and deserve to be punished. But with You there is mercy and unfailing love, and we thank You for forgiving our sins. Help us act as You want us to, for Jesus' sake. Amen.

[God says,] *"Return to Me, for I have redeemed you."*
Isaiah 44:22

We Belong to God

Jeremiah's dog ran away. He ended up in a yard down the street. The boy who lived there locked the dog in his garage.

One day Jeremiah was walking down the alley. He heard a dog barking inside a garage. Jeremiah looked through the garage window and saw his dog.

But Jeremiah knew that the boy who lived there would not give his dog back. So he told the boy, "I'll give you $5.00 for that dog." The boy wanted the $5.00 more than the dog, so he sold the dog to Jeremiah. Jeremiah bought him back. That's what "redeem" means—to buy back.

Do you know that we, too, were bought back? God made us, and we belong to Him. But like everybody else, we ran away from God. We didn't love Him and we did wrong things. We call that sinning. When people sin, the devil tries to keep them with him. Those who belong to the devil can't get away from him by themselves.

But God bought us back. He redeemed us. Like Jeremiah, God paid for us. When Jesus died for us on the cross, that was the price He paid to get us back as His children. Jesus, our Savior, saved us from sin and from the devil. God says in the Bible, "Return to Me, for I have redeemed you."

$\approx$

Let's talk: What happened to Jeremiah's dog? How did Jeremiah get his dog back? To whom do all people belong? When does the devil get hold of people? What did Jesus do to buy us back for God? Who returned us to God?

Older children and adults may read: Isaiah 44:21–23

Let's pray: Thank You, God, for redeeming us and taking us back even though we often run away from You and sin. Help us remember how much You paid to have us as Your children. We ask this in Jesus' name. Amen.

Live in peace. And the God of love and peace will be with you. 2 Corinthians 13:11

Getting Along with Others

Have you ever set up dominoes or small blocks of wood one behind the other? When the front block is pushed over, the whole row falls down. Why? Because each block hits the next one as it falls.

There's a way of stopping the whole row from falling—just take one block out of the row. Then the hitting and falling will stop.

An argument is like a row of dominoes. One person's words hit at the next person's words, and they fall over each other. Do you know how to stop an argument? Take out one angry bunch of words that hits at what the other person says. Say something friendly instead, or just don't say anything. See if that stops the argument.

Jesus said to His friends and followers, "Have peace with one another." That means, "Get along with one another." Our Bible verse says, "Live in peace." The opposite of peace is fighting and arguing, which is fighting with words.

Is it possible to live in peace with everybody? How about the boy who tries to start an argument? Or the girl who's always stirring up trouble? It can be difficult to avoid trouble. But the Bible says, "If it is possible, as much as you can, live in peace with everybody." God wants us to try to get along with others.

God is love, and God loves peace. When Jesus lives in our hearts, we can love others and try to live in peace. And the Bible says the God of love and peace has promised to be with us.

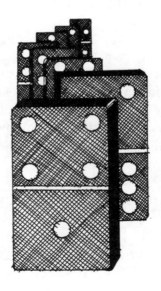

Let's talk: What does it mean to "have peace" or to "live in peace" with one another? How can we usually stop a fight? Who helps us live in peace with others? Why is God called the God of love and peace?

Older children and adults may read: Romans 12:14–21

Let's pray: Dear Father in heaven, please forgive all the fighting we have done. Be with us in our hearts so that we can live in peace with other people. We ask this because we are Your children. In Jesus' name. Amen.

[We] should always pray and not give up. Luke 18:1

Why Keep On Praying?

There was once a judge who didn't care about people at all. He didn't even care about God. One day a widow came to him. "Please help me," she begged. "My enemy is trying to harm me."

The judge said, "Don't bother me. I don't have time for you." So the widow went away.

The next day, the widow came back to the judge and asked for his help again. Once more he told her to go home. But she came back the next day and the next day and the next day. She kept coming day after day. She did not leave him alone. She didn't give up asking.

At last the judge said, "I don't care about God, and I don't care about this widow. But because she keeps on bothering me, I will help her; otherwise she will wear me out." The judge helped her so she would stop coming to him for help.

After Jesus told this story, He said, "Remember what this uncaring judge said and did. Won't God give help to His own people who keep on praying to Him day and night? I tell you, He will hurry to help them."

So Jesus told us to keep on praying, even when God doesn't seem to help us right away. God loves us and will answer our prayers much more quickly than the judge who helped the widow.

Let's talk: What did the widow ask the judge? Why didn't the judge want to help her? Why did he finally help her? Why did Jesus tell the story about the widow and the judge? Why will God always help us? Why doesn't He always help us right away?

Older children and adults may read: Luke 18:1–8

Let's pray: Dear Lord, please help us in all our troubles. Teach us to pray to You for help and to keep on praying. We know that You love us, and we're glad You have promised to answer our prayers. Please hear our prayers for Jesus' sake. Amen.

Jesus … went around doing good. Acts 10:38

Imitating Jesus

Boy Scouts are asked to do one good deed every day. Do you think Jesus was satisfied with doing only one good deed a day? The Bible says, "Jesus … went around doing good." Wherever He went, Jesus did good; and whatever He did was good.

What are some of the good things Jesus did?

Jesus worked. He was a carpenter. He made things that other people could use. Jesus wants us to work. You can help your parents by helping around the house. You can do your homework without being told. Jesus will help you do your work well.

Jesus healed the sick. We can't heal the sick, but we can pray for them, cheer them up, and help them in other ways. You might even become a doctor or a nurse.

When people were hungry, Jesus gave them something to eat. Jesus wants us to feed the hungry. He said that when we give food to hungry people because we love Him, we are doing good to Him.

Jesus taught people about God. Jesus talked to people about His Father in heaven and about Himself and how people could become God's children. We can take people to

Sunday school and church and give people Bibles and other books that tell the Good News about Jesus, our Savior.

Jesus went around doing good. And Jesus promises to help us do good, too.

Let's talk: What does our Bible verse say Jesus did wherever He went? What were some good things Jesus did? How can we help the sick? How can we help people learn more about God and the way to heaven? Why do Christians want to do good?

Older children and adults may read: Acts 10:36–43

Let's pray: Dear heavenly Father, we want to be like Jesus. Forgive us for not doing as much good as we can. Help us grow up doing good as Jesus did. In His name we ask this. Amen.

Let us not become weary in doing good. Galatians 6:9

Don't Quit Doing Good

A man on television was helping people get jobs. Out of the first thousand people for whom he got jobs, how many do you think said thank you? Only 10. Should he quit trying to help people just because they weren't thankful?

Jesus once passed by a place where there were 10 men sick with leprosy. Doctors in Jesus' time weren't able to heal people with this disease. There was no hope for these men. They begged Jesus to help them, and Jesus did. He healed them. But how many came back to say thank You to Jesus? Only one. Did Jesus quit doing good because people weren't thankful?

Jesus never gets tired of being good to people. To whom does He still do good? To you and me and everyone else in the world, even though we often forget to thank Him. We even disobey Him in many ways every day. You'd think He would get tired of doing good for us. But He keeps right on forgiving us and loving us and helping us.

So why should we get tired of helping other people? "Let us not become weary [or tired] in doing good," the Bible says. If people don't appreciate what we do for them, remember that most people didn't thank Jesus either, and they still don't. Even we don't. But Jesus keeps right on being good to everyone. And He will help us keep doing good if we ask Him.

Let's talk: How many people said thanks to the man on the television? How many of the men Jesus healed from leprosy came back to thank Him? Who never gets tired of doing good? What does the Bible verse tell us?

Older children and adults may read: Galatians 6:1–10

Let's pray: Dear Jesus, we're glad that You never get tired of doing good to us. Please help us show our thanks by never getting tired of doing good for other people. Amen.

Get rid of all bitterness, … and anger. Ephesians 4:31

Something to Get Rid Of

When Brian didn't get what he wanted right away, he'd scream. If his mother didn't come running, he screamed even louder. If Brian screamed hard enough and loud enough and got red in the face, his mother would do anything he wanted.

Brian learned to get his way by becoming angry and screaming. He would lose his temper whenever his friends didn't do what he wanted. He would yell mean things, even about his friends, when they didn't do what he wanted.

Brian grew up and got married. He always had to have his way. When his wife and children didn't obey him, he threw things at them, yelled at them, and hit them. His wife was afraid of him, and his children didn't love him.

What if God, our Father in heaven, were like Brian? What if God became angry and punished us every time we didn't do what He wants? He'd be punishing us all the time, wouldn't He?

But the Bible says, "The Lord is slow to become angry." Because God is good and full of love, He is kind and forgiving. He sent His Son, Jesus, to die for us on the cross so that He wouldn't have to punish us. And Jesus rose again and makes us God's dear children.

God wants His children to be like Him. That's why He says, "Get rid of all bitterness … and anger."

Let's talk: What did Brian do to get his way when he was little? Why were his wife and children afraid of him? What if God became angry at us for not doing what He wants? Why is God slow to become angry and willing to forgive us? How does He want us to treat others?

Older children and adults may read: Psalm 145:1–8

Let's pray: Dear Lord God, it is wonderful to know that You are full of love and slow to become angry. Continue to love us for the sake of Jesus, our Savior. Help us to get rid of all anger and mean talk. In Jesus' name we ask this. Amen.

You shall not steal. Exodus 20:15

God's Law Is Good

"Why is it wrong to steal?" Yuri asked his mother. "I wish it were all right to steal. Then I could take candy from the store when I want to."

That night Yuri had a dream. He dreamed that it wasn't wrong to steal. In his dream, he went to a store and took some candy. He also took some apples and some potato chips.

The next day he went to the store again. It was empty. People had taken everything. The store owner had locked the store and put up a sign. It said, "For sale." Nobody wanted to buy the store because when it was open, people just took whatever they wanted.

In his dream Yuri went home. He asked his mother for an ice-cream cone. "We can't get any ice cream," said his mother. "All the ice cream has been stolen. No one sells ice cream anymore."

Then Yuri went out to ride his bike. It was gone. He ran back into the house. "Mother," he cried, "somebody stole my bike."

"Remember, it's all right to steal what belongs to somebody else," his mother said.

Yuri started to cry even harder. He didn't like what stealing did to him. He wished everybody would obey God's commandment. He didn't want to live in a world where stealing was okay.

Yuri woke up. It was only a dream. He looked out the window. His bike was in the yard. "Mother, I don't ever want to steal anything," he said.

"I'm glad," said his mother. "God knows what's best for us. That's why He told us not to steal."

Let's talk: Which commandment did Yuri want to change? What happened in his dream? Who gave us the commandment, "You shall not steal"? Why is it a good commandment? What does the Bible call the breaking of God's commandments?

Older children and adults may read: Romans 2:21–24

Let's pray: Thank You for giving us Your commandments, dear God. Help us keep them. When we do break them, forgive us for Jesus' sake. In His name we pray. Amen.

[Jesus said,] "You are the salt of the earth." Matthew 5:13

What Good Does Salt Do?

"Noah is a pickle-puss," said Julia.

"And Julia is a salt barrel," said Noah. They were just teasing; they weren't fighting.

"I know I'm salt," said Julia. "And so are you. Jesus said so."

"He did?" asked Noah, a little surprised. "When did He say that?"

"Jesus told His followers, 'You are the salt of the earth,' " Julia told Noah. "Jesus meant that about us, too, didn't He, Dad?" Julia asked as their father walked into the room.

"Yes, He meant all of His disciples, and that includes the people who believe in Him and love Him today," Dad answered. "But do you know how we are to be salt?"

Julia and Noah didn't know. They asked Dad to explain. "Well, when I was a boy living on the farm, your grandmother had a pork barrel," Dad said. "We didn't have a refrigerator, so she put our meat into the barrel. Then she put a lot of salt on it. The salt kept the meat from getting rotten. It kept the worms out.

"Jesus wants us to keep the people around us from getting rotten," Dad continued. "When we live as Jesus wants us to live, we are like the good salt that Jesus wants us to be."

⁓

Let's talk: What did the salt in the pork barrel do? Why did Jesus call His followers "salt"? How are we like salt to people around us? How does Jesus keep people from becoming rotten? Memorize the Bible verse.

Older children and adults may read: Matthew 5:13–16

Let's pray: Dear Jesus, we want to be like salt. Help us to show many people Your love. Make each of us a Christian example for all those around us. Amen.

I will dwell in the house of the Lord forever. Psalm 23:6

Going to God's House

Mrs. Rains was crying because her daughter Amber had died. For the funeral, they put Amber in a pretty box. Later they took her to the cemetery. There they put her down in a grave. She would never come back to play or hug her mother and say, "I love you." She was dead. So Mrs. Rains cried.

"Don't cry, Margery," Mr. Rains said. "Amber is in heaven. It's only her body that's dead. Amber is in the house of the Lord. It's a beautiful place. And Jesus is there with her, taking good care of her."

"Yes, I know," said Mrs. Rains, and she tried to smile. "But I miss her."

"We'll see her again when we go to the house of the Lord," said Mr. Rains.

As Mr. and Mrs. Rains grew older, they often prayed, "Dear Jesus, please take us to Your home in heaven someday. We want to be with You and Amber always." And they knew Jesus would take them to His house.

Mr. and Mrs. Rains often said Psalm 23 together. They liked the last words best of all, "I will dwell in the house of the Lord forever." When they said these words, they thought of Amber and the time when they would be with her and Jesus in heaven.

Let's talk: What happened to Amber? Where did Jesus take Amber when she died? When did Amber's parents expect to see her again? Why is heaven called "the house of the Lord"? Memorize the Bible verse.

Older children and adults may read: Psalm 23

Let's pray: Thank You, Lord Jesus, for all that You have done so that we can be in heaven with You someday. We thank You for dying on the cross to save us. Thank You for being our Savior so that we can live with You forever in heaven. Amen.

In the day of my trouble I will call to You, for You will answer me. Psalm 86:7

Jesus Always Helps

"I'm afraid to tell Mr. Griffin that I broke his garage window," said Allan. He and his friends had been throwing rocks at cans on Mr. Griffin's fence posts. One of Allan's stones had gone too far.

"You're in real trouble, aren't you?" said his sister, Trina. "Did he see you?"

"No, but I keep thinking about it," Allan said. "Jesus knows I did it. But if I tell Mr. Griffin, he may get angry."

"Why don't you ask Jesus what to do?" Trina suggested.

"I already know what He wants me to do," Allan admitted. "He wants me to tell the truth and pay for the window. But how can I?"

"Why don't you ask Jesus to help you?" Trina said.

Allan decided to pray to Jesus. "Dear Jesus, help me do what's right," he prayed. Then he went over to Mr. Griffin's house and knocked on the door.

Mr. Griffin came to the door. "We were throwing rocks and one of mine broke your garage window," Allan admitted. "I'm very sorry, and I'll pay for it."

"Well, I'm glad you told me," Mr. Griffin said. "A man is coming today to put on new storm windows. I'll have him replace the garage window first. You can pay me when you have the money."

Allan felt much better when he heard that. He thanked Mr. Griffin, and on the way home, he thanked Jesus. He knew that Jesus had helped him do what was right and that Jesus had made it turn out all right.

Let's talk: What was Allan's problem? What did Trina tell him to do? What was the right thing for Allan to do? Why? How did Jesus help Allan do what was right? How did it turn out?

Older children and adults may read: Psalm 86:3–12

Let's pray: Thank You, dear Jesus, for always helping us when we call on You. We thank You especially for helping us get out of the trouble of sin by forgiving us. We love You for that. Amen.

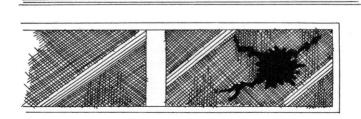

Now we are children of God. 1 John 3:2

God's Children

There was once a poor orphan girl who, like Cinderella, had to work hard for the people with whom she lived. She had to do the things nobody else wanted to do. And she wasn't paid very much for what she did.

One day a king and his son visited the farm where the girl lived. The king's son fell in love with the girl. "Don't tell anybody," he told her. "Someday I'll come back and marry you."

The girl kept right on doing her work, but now she was happy and cheerful and sang all day long. Nobody knew why she was so happy, but she knew: She was going to marry a prince and become the child of the king.

We are all like that girl. For a while we live here on earth. We may have hard work and many troubles. But Jesus, God's Son, came to earth to suffer and die so God could adopt us as His children. Jesus has promised to come back and take us to our Father's home in heaven? So we can be happy waiting for Jesus.

"Now we are children of God," says the Bible, and that's wonderful to know. But the Bible says it will be even more wonderful when we are with Jesus in heaven.

Let's talk: Why was the orphan girl happy even though she had to work hard? Whose Son came from heaven and promised to take us there? Because Jesus loves us and has saved us from sin, what does the heavenly Father call us?

Older children and adults may read: 1 John 3:1–5

Let's pray: Dear God, we're glad that You call us Your children for Jesus' sake. We know that Jesus is coming to take us to heaven. Help us remember this so that we will be happy while we wait. We ask this in Jesus' name. Amen.

How great are Your works, O Lord. Psalm 92:5

God Is Great and Good

In California there was a man who studied the stars. He looked through a gigantic telescope and saw that there were millions of stars, some much bigger than the earth. Some of these stars moved around, but they never bumped into one another. Every star had its own place or path. The man could tell where any star would be a year later. The man said, "Surely this is the work of God. Who else could have planned all this?"

Another man studied germs. He put a drop of water under a microscope. The microscope made the drop of water look almost as big as a dinner plate. Through the microscope, the man could see all kinds of tiny bugs swimming around in the drop of water. "Look at those germs," he said. "Millions of them in a drop of water. And they all live until it's time for them to die. How great are Your works, O Lord!"

A young woman rode on a train through the Rocky Mountains. As she looked out of the window, she said, "How great are Your works, O Lord!"

A boy caught some snow on his gloves. He noticed that every flake of snow was different. He remembered the words, "How great are Your works, O Lord!"

These are just a few of the people who understood and believed what the psalm writer said long ago in the Bible. And the greatest thing God ever did was send His Son, Jesus, to be our Savior. "How great are Your works, O Lord!"

⮵

Let's talk: What did one man see through a telescope? What did another see in a drop of water? What great work of God did a young woman see from a train window? What made the boy think of God? What is the greatest work God has done for us?

Older children and adults may read: Psalm 92:1–5

Let's pray: All that You have ever done, Lord God, shows how great You are. We praise You for all Your wonderful works. We especially thank and praise You for sending Jesus to die for us and for bringing Him back to life on the first Easter. Keep us as Your dear children every day for Jesus' sake. Amen.

How sweet are Your words to my taste, sweeter than honey to my mouth! Psalm 119:103

God's Word Is Sweet

A man stood on the side of a high bridge. His life was full of problems. He and his little boy had been in a car accident, and his little boy died. His wife blamed him and wouldn't live with him anymore. The man didn't think anybody loved him, so he had decided to jump off the bridge. That's how bad he felt.

As he stood looking down at the water, a car came across the bridge. On the bumper were three words, "God loves you."

The man sat down and cried. He cried because he was happy. He remembered a Bible verse he had learned in Sunday school. "God so loved the world that He gave His one and only Son." He remembered his teacher saying Jesus loved him so much that He gave His life to save him.

That man tasted how sweet the Word of God is. When a man in a desert doesn't have water for two days and then finds water, how good the water tastes to him! When a person thinks that nobody loves her and then remembers how Jesus died for her, that's when God's words seem extra sweet, sweeter than honey.

But all of God's children love to hear and learn God's Word. They want to hear and learn more about Jesus, their Savior. God's words are sweet, and to those who love Jesus, they seem sweeter than honey.

Let's talk: What was the man on the bridge going to do? Why? Why did he cry? When does God's Word seem extra sweet to people? Why do God's children love His Word? What is your favorite Bible verse?

Older children and adults may read: Psalm 119:97–104

Let's pray: Thank You, dear Father in heaven, for the sweet message that You love us and have made us Your children. Your promises of forgiveness and life in heaven are sweeter than honey. Teach us to love Your words. Make us want to learn more and more of them and never forget them. We ask this in Jesus' name. Amen.

*"With everlasting kindness I will have compassion on you,"
says the Lord your Redeemer.* Isaiah 54:8

God's Kindness Never Stops

Erica loved to visit Mrs. Howell, the lady who lived next door. Mrs. Howell talked to Erica and gave her cookies and soda.

One day, Erica stepped off the porch and right on top of Mrs. Howell's best flowers. "I didn't mean to," Erica said.

But Mrs. Howell became very angry. "Get out of here," she told Erica. "And don't ever come back."

Erica ran home. She was scared and upset. She ran and told her father what Mrs. Howell had said.

"I'm glad to hear it was an accident," said Dad. "I'll go and talk to Mrs. Howell. Maybe we can get her some new flowers."

"She was so nice on other days," said Erica. "Why would she be so mean all of a sudden?"

"Oh, she just lost her temper," Dad said. "Aren't you glad that God isn't like that? The Bible says His kindness lasts forever."

"Jesus would have said, 'I know you didn't mean to do it, Erica,' and He would have forgiven me," said Erica.

"Yes, I'm sure He would have," Dad agreed. "He forgives us many things every day, and His kindness never ends."

Let's talk: What did Mrs. Howell say to Erica when she stepped on her flowers? What did Erica's father say he would do? Who never stops being kind and forgiving? What did Erica think Jesus would have said to her?

Older children and adults may read: Isaiah 54:7–13

Let's pray: Thank You, dear Lord, our loving God, for always being kind to us and ready to forgive us. Please help us always to be kind and loving to others for Jesus' sake. Amen.

The Lord's will be done. Acts 21:14

Letting God Decide Things

It wasn't any fun to be in jail in the days when the apostle Paul was preaching about Jesus. Jails were like dirty cellars, and prisoners were treated roughly.

One time Paul was on his way to Jerusalem. On the way, he stopped to visit a friend. There the prophet Agabus came to see him. He took Paul's belt and tied his own hands and feet with it. Then he said, "The Holy Spirit has told me that the people in Jerusalem will tie up the man who owns this belt and will give him to the soldiers."

Then the friends of Paul said to him, "Don't go to Jerusalem. Please don't go."

But Paul said, "What are you trying to do by crying and breaking my heart? I want God's will to be done, even if I have to go to jail. I'm even willing to die for Jesus."

When the friends of Paul saw that he wouldn't change his mind, they quit begging him not to go. They said, "The Lord's will be done."

Sometimes we wish things could be different from what they are. We can ask God to change things, but sometimes His answer is no or wait awhile. Sometimes we don't know what's best. But God always knows what's best, so we can always say, "The Lord's will be done." Whatever He wants is best for us because He loves us.

$$\approx$$

Let's talk: What did the prophet Agabus say would happen to Paul? What did Paul's friends beg him not to do? What did Paul say he was willing to do for Jesus' sake? When the friends of Paul saw that they couldn't keep him from going to Jerusalem, what did they say? Why are Christians willing to let God decide things?

Older children and adults may read: Acts 21:10–15

Let's pray: Dear Lord God, help us say, "The Lord's will be done," no matter what may happen to us. As long as You decide things for us, we know that everything will turn out all right. Amen.

He who is kind to the poor lends to the Lord, and He will reward him for what he has done. Proverbs 19:17

What God Wants to Borrow

On his first trip to New York City, Todd couldn't help but stare at all the wonderful sights. He saw the Empire State Building, the Statue of Liberty, the World Trade Center, and even Central Park. Everywhere Todd and his family went, they walked with huge crowds of people. And everywhere the family turned, it seemed they saw someone begging, or asking for food, or offering to do something in exchange for a little money.

"Mom, why are those people asking for money? Why don't they have any?" Todd asked. "Can't they get a job?"

"Well, honey, some of these people make a lot of money begging on the streets," Mom answered. "They don't want to work. But a lot of these people have lost their jobs and homes and even their families. They need our help."

It's true that some people ask for things they don't really need. But there are many people in this world who are poor and have no way to feed themselves or their families, buy clothing, or find a home to live in. These are the people we are to help as if we were helping Jesus Himself.

There are people all around us who need our help. Does your church have a food pantry or a clothing drive? Do you collect toys or winter clothes at Christmas? Can your family volunteer at a shelter during Thanksgiving or Easter?

When we give money, food, clothing, or our time to help others, it's the same as if we were giving to the Lord. God's Word says, "He who is kind to the poor lends to the Lord." And what we give to the Lord, He will pay back to us in many ways.

Let's talk: Do you know of someone who may need your help? What can you do for them? To whom do we lend when we give to the poor? What does God promise to do for those who are kind to the poor?

Older children and adults may read: Deuteronomy 24:19–21

Let's pray: Thank You for all the good things we have received from You, dear Father in heaven. Please give us loving hearts so that we will gladly help those in need. We ask this in Jesus' name. Amen.

I have no greater joy than to hear that my children are walking in the truth. 3 John 4

Happy People

"How are you, my boy?" asked Mr. Timmons.

"Great," called André as he ran up the steps into his house.

"Mom, why does Mr. Timmons call me his boy? I'm not his boy," André said as he put his backpack on the kitchen table.

"Oh, many grown-up people talk that way," said Mom. "It means that he likes you, as if you were his son."

In our Bible verse, the disciple John was writing to people who weren't his children, but he called them his children. He loved them as though they were his children. And in one way they were his children. He had taught them God's Word. He had been their pastor and teacher.

One day John received a letter that said the Christians he had taught in Ephesus were kind to the poor. That made him very happy. Then somebody told John that his church members were good to the people who were working for Jesus. That also made him happy. John knew by their actions that the Christians in Ephesus loved Jesus. That's why he wrote, "I have no greater joy than to hear that my children are walking in the truth."

To walk in the truth means to do what God says. It means believing and doing what the Bible teaches. Our ministers and teachers and our parents are glad, too, when they see their "children" walk in the truth. Nothing makes them happier than to see their children living as Christians.

But we walk in the truth only if we keep learning the truth. That's why it's so important for us to study the

Bible in our home, to go to Sunday school, to attend a Christian day school and high school if we can, and to go to church together every time we can.

⁓

Let's talk: What are some things people believe when they walk in the truth? What are some things they do? In what book can we find the truth about Jesus and His teachings? Who helps us live as Christians? How do others who love Jesus feel when they see that we love Him?

Older children and adults may read: 3 John 2–4, 11

Let's pray: Dear Jesus, help us follow You, for we know that You are the only true Way to heaven. Keep us as Your children so that our parents and all who love You will always be happy about us. Amen.

Serve one another in love. Galatians 5:13

Serving Others As Jesus Did

"Mommy, please get me a drink of water," asked Nicole. She was sick in bed. Mommy was glad to do it. She served Nicole by getting her a glass of water.

When Nicole was better, she asked, "Mommy, please get me a drink of water." This time she could have gotten it herself, but she didn't want to walk into the kitchen.

"I think you can get your own glass of water now that you're better," said Mommy. "I don't want you to learn to depend on others for things you can do yourself. The Bible tells us to serve one another. That means we should be ready to help others, not always wait to be helped."

So Nicole got the drink of water herself. "Mommy, do you want one too?" she asked.

"Yes, I would. Thank you, Nicole, for thinking of me," answered Mommy. She was glad that Nicole was willing to serve.

God wants us to be helpful to other people, to love them enough to serve them. Jesus said that to become great in His kingdom, we must serve others. After all, Jesus gave His life for us, and we are to be imitators of Him.

⁓

Let's talk: How did Nicole's mother serve her when she was sick? Why didn't she serve Nicole once she was better? What does *serve* mean? What does our Bible verse tell us? How did Jesus serve people when He was on earth? What did He say was the only way to become great?

Older children and adults may read: Matthew 20:25–28

Let's pray: Dear Jesus, we know that You died on the cross to serve us. We want to love other people enough to help them. Forgive us for the times we want to be served instead of wanting to serve others. In Your name we pray. Amen.

[Jesus] came to seek and to save what was lost. Luke 19:10

Helping Jesus Save the Lost

David had gone just a short way into the woods, but now he couldn't find his way out. He cried and called, but nobody answered. He was lost.

Then David told himself to stay right where he was. Somebody will come looking for me, he thought. I know my dad will, he reassured himself.

David went to the top of a hill and sat down. Soon he heard his dad calling him. David was so happy to be found!

Many people are far away from God and are lost. They think they're going to heaven, but they're going the wrong way. Jesus is looking for them. He came to find the lost people and save them.

Jesus has found us and saved us. Without Him, we would all be lost. Every time we sin, we walk away from God. But Jesus calls us back. He even died for us on the cross to save us. Because Jesus rose again, we have the promise of eternal life with Him in heaven when we die.

Many people don't know about Jesus, and some don't care. They're still lost. Jesus wants to find them. He wants to save them, too. But how does Jesus save these people? Through those of us who have already been found. He does it when we tell others that Jesus is their Savior. Those who believe us and follow Jesus are saved. They are brought back to God.

Let's talk: How was David lost? How do people become lost on the way to heaven? What did Jesus do to save all people? How do we know whether Jesus has found us? How do we help save others who are lost?

Older children and adults may read: Luke 19:1–10

Let's pray: Dear Jesus, we're glad that You found us and are taking us to heaven. We want to help find others who are lost so that they, too, will be saved. Please help us. In Your name. Amen.

But Jesus immediately said to them: "Take courage! It is I. Don't be afraid." Matthew 14:27

Don't Be Afraid

Angelica screamed. She was having a nightmare. In her dream, a big, ugly dragon came out of the clouds. She thought it was going to eat her.

Aunt Claire woke her up and said, "Don't be afraid, Angelica. I'm here, and you're all right."

But Angelica was afraid to go back to sleep. So Aunt Claire told her the story about Jesus walking on the water. She explained how Jesus' friends were sailing across a lake. A big storm blew across the water. The disciples were having trouble keeping the boat from sinking. It was dark. Suddenly they saw someone walking on the water.

The disciples were afraid, Aunt Claire told Angelica. They thought it was a ghost who would hurt them. Then the disciples heard a voice. It said, "Take courage! It is I. Don't be afraid."

At first the disciples didn't believe it was Jesus. But when Jesus came into their boat, they were happy.

"Angelica, we sometimes see scary things in a dream, just like Jesus' friends did during the storm," Aunt Claire said. "But when the disciples knew that Jesus was with them, they weren't afraid anymore.

"Jesus is right by our bed, even in the dark," Aunt Claire continued. "He's with us, no matter where we are. And when we're afraid, Jesus says to us, 'Take courage … don't be afraid.' "

"I'm not afraid anymore," Angelica said. And she put her head back on the pillow and was soon fast asleep.

Let's talk: What scared Angelica? What scared Jesus' friends? What sometimes scares people today? Where is Jesus whenever we're afraid? What did Jesus say when His friends were afraid? Why can Jesus always help us? How can we help anybody who is afraid?

Older children and adults may read: Matthew 14:22–33

Let's pray: Dear Jesus, please help us when we're afraid. Remind us that You are always with us and that You won't let anything hurt us. Then we won't worry. We know that You love us. Amen.

[Peter asked,] "How many times shall I forgive my brother when he sins against me? Up to seven times?" Matthew 18:21

Seventy-Seven Times

"I'm never going to speak to him again," Hope yelled as she stomped into the family room. She was angry because her brother, Evan, had called her a fat cat.

"Aren't God's children supposed to forgive one another?" Dad asked.

"I'm tired of forgiving him," Hope replied. "Why do I always have to forgive?"

"Hope, did you know that the disciple Peter once asked Jesus, 'How many times shall I forgive my brother when he sins against me? Up to seven times?' What do you think Jesus answered?" Dad asked. "Jesus said, 'Not seven times, but 77 times.' "

Why do you think Jesus said 77 times? He meant we should always be willing to forgive, no matter how often somebody does something wrong against us. After all, Jesus forgives us every time we sin.

Jesus told Peter this story:

"Once there was a man who owed his king more than he could ever pay back. So the king decided to sell the man and his wife and children as slaves. But when the man begged the king not to do it, the king forgave his debt and said he wouldn't have to pay anything at all.

As the man left the king's palace, he saw someone who owed him only a small amount. Because he couldn't pay the debt, the man put him in prison. When the king heard about this, he became angry. He had his soldiers bring the unkind man back to him. The king said, 'You wicked servant, I canceled all that you owed me. Shouldn't you have had mercy on your fellow servant just as I had on you?' Then the king put the man in jail until he could pay back everything he owed.

Then Jesus said, "This is how My heavenly Father will treat each of you unless you forgive your brother from your heart." Our Father in heaven forgives our sins and He expects us to do the same for other people.

⁓

Let's talk: What did Peter think would be enough times to forgive someone? How often does Jesus say we are to forgive? What did Jesus mean when He said, "Seventy-seven times"? How much did the king forgive the unkind servant? How much has God forgiven us? Why was the servant punished?

Older children and adults may read: Matthew 18:23–35

Let's pray: Dear heavenly Father, we're thankful that You have forgiven us thousands of times and that You are always willing to forgive us for Jesus' sake. Please give us Your Holy Spirit so that we will always be willing to forgive other people for Jesus' sake. Amen.

Jesus answered ... "Anyone who has seen Me has seen the Father." John 14:9

Seeing What God Is Like

Sumiko and Amanda were in Amanda's back yard one summer night. Each girl had a flashlight and was shining it into dark places. Suddenly, Sumiko pointed hers toward the sky. "I wish I could see God," she said.

Amanda pointed her flashlight up, too. "So do I," she said.

While Jesus was on earth, His friend Philip wanted to see God. He said to Jesus, "Lord, show us the Father and that will be enough for us."

Jesus answered, "Anyone who has seen Me has seen the Father." Jesus, the Son of God, is exactly like His Father, so those who know Jesus know what God is like.

What was Jesus like when He was on earth? The Bible tells us He was kind. He loved children. He could do anything. He helped people. Jesus taught people about life with God. He even died on the cross so we can live with Him in heaven.

Have you ever wanted to see God? We can't see Him with our human eyes, but we can see Him with the eyes of faith. Jesus said, "Anyone who has seen Me has seen the Father." We can see what Jesus—and God the Father—is like by hearing and learning about Jesus.

Let's talk: Whom did Sumiko and Amanda wish they could see? What did Jesus tell His friend Philip when he asked to see God? How can we get to know Jesus? What was Jesus like when He was on earth? Memorize the Bible verse.

Older children and adults may read: John 14:6–12

Let's pray: Dear God, we know how kind Jesus is and how much He loves us. We're glad that You are just like Him. Help us learn more about Him so that we will know You better and love You more. We ask this as Your dear children. Amen.

Like newborn babies, crave pure spiritual milk, so that by it you may grow up in your salvation. 1 Peter 2:2

What Makes Christians Grow?

"How tall am I now, Mom?" Scott asked almost every day. He wanted to grow faster. Sometimes Mom would have him stand against a wall and measure him. Then Scott would stand on his tiptoes to be as tall as possible.

"Eat your vegetables and drink your milk, and God will make you grow big and strong," said Mom.

Vegetables and milk do help us grow tall, but tall is not the only way to grow. God wants us to grow in our knowledge and love of Him. He wants us to become grown-up Christians. The Bible says, "Grow in the grace and knowledge of our Lord and Savior Jesus Christ."

How can we grow in knowing the Lord? We grow when we learn Bible stories and verses and believe what they tell us about Jesus. We grow when we go to Sunday school and church. We grow when we listen to the pastor and when we have family devotions every day. We grow when we live as Jesus wants us to. We grow when we talk about God with our parents, teachers, and friends.

So you see, we grow in the knowledge of Jesus by learning God's Word. Our Bible verse says that God's Word is like milk. This milk helps us grow as Christians. That's why we want it just like babies want milk. Milk makes us grow. And so does the Word of God.

Let's talk: What helps our body grow? How can we grow in knowing the Lord Jesus? What's as important as knowing about Jesus and His teachings? Who helps us grow up Christians?

Older children and adults may read: Acts 18:24–26

Let's pray: Dear Lord Jesus, we want to grow up as Christians. Please bless our Bible lessons so that we will learn to know You better. And give us Your Holy Spirit to help us always love You and become more and more like You. Amen.

Whatever is lovely, whatever is admirable ... think about such things. Philippians 4:8

What to Think About

There is a story about a mean, ugly man. He didn't like beautiful things, and he lived all alone in a dark old house.

Then one day the man fell in love with a beautiful woman. He wanted to marry her, but she said, "I won't marry a man whose face isn't beautiful."

So the man bought a mask that made him look like a kind and caring person. He also did his best to treat the woman with kindness. Together they did many wonderful things. They read books together. They listened to beautiful music. They walked together in the parks and enjoyed God's beautiful birds and flowers.

Eventually, they were married, and they were very happy. But one day an enemy came to the man's house. He tore the mask off the man's face in front of his wife. The man tried to hide his face. He didn't want his wife to see how ugly he was. But when he looked in a mirror, he saw that his face had become beautiful like the person he had tried to be.

This isn't a true story, but it has a true meaning. The Bible tells us to think of things that are lovely and good.

When we do this, we become more and more like Jesus because He is in our mind and in our heart.

Let's talk: What changed the mean man's face? What does God want His children to think about? How can we tell what is in some people's minds and hearts? How can having Jesus in our heart change the way we look? Why does God want us to think of things that are good and lovely?

Older children and adults may read: Philippians 4:4–9

Let's pray: Dear Father in heaven, we know that You are good and that everything You think and do is good. We thank You for loving us and sending Jesus to save us from our sins. Please help us to be the kind of people You want us to be, through Jesus, our Savior. Amen.

Love is kind. 1 Corinthians 13:4

What Love Does

"Dad, Chandra has a new haircut and does it ever look funny," Haley laughed as she walked in the front door.

"Funny?" asked Dad. "What makes it look funny?"

"Oh, I don't know," Haley replied. "Christa said it was funny, so we all laughed about it."

"I was out in the yard when Chandra walked by on her way home from school. She was crying. Don't you think you probably hurt Chandra's feelings when you laughed at her?" her dad asked.

Haley dropped her eyes. She suddenly felt ashamed. She knew she'd been unkind.

"I thought Chandra's new haircut looked very nice. It made her eyes look very pretty," Dad continued. "Perhaps Christa was jealous. In any case, do you like being laughed at?"

"No," was all Haley could say. She felt like crying too.

"Do you remember what Jesus told us about treating others the way we want to be treated?" Dad asked. "We all want to be treated with love and kindness. And love is kind. People who love try not to hurt one another."

Do you know what Haley did? She went to Chandra's house and told her how pretty her new haircut was. Haley was sorry she had made fun of Chandra.

~

Let's talk: How were the girls at school unkind to Chandra? What makes us unkind to some people? Who wants us to love other people the way we love ourselves? What kind words could the girls have said to Chandra? Memorize the Bible verse.

Older children and adults may read: 1 Corinthians 13:4–7

Let's pray: Dear Father in heaven, we're often thoughtless and unkind to others. Please forgive us for Jesus' sake. We know that He died for these sins. Help us treat others as we want to be treated—with love. In Jesus' name we ask this. Amen.

God loves a cheerful giver. 2 Corinthians 9:7

What Kind of Giver Are You?

DeShawn wasn't a cheerful giver. He always wanted his gifts back. For example, he gave Brandon a basketball. After a while, DeShawn wanted it back. Sometimes his friends wouldn't give his gifts back. That made DeShawn angry. He would even scream and fight to get them back.

Deka was different. She liked to give things to others. Friends said she was generous. Deka realized that when she gave things, the gifts made people happy. And giving made her happy too.

In Sunday school, DeShawn and Deka heard about some children who didn't know about God. "You don't have to give anything, but anyone who wants to may bring some money to help send missionaries to Africa," Mrs. Marshall, their teacher, said. "The missionaries will tell the children in Africa about Jesus and His love."

That week Deka asked her mother if she could do some extra chores around the house to earn some money. She wanted to take $3 for the missionaries and her allowance was only $1.50. Mother gladly gave Deka some extra things to do. When their neighbor heard about Deka's Sunday school project, she gave Deka $5 for watering her flowers and sweeping her sidewalk after school.

The next Sunday morning, DeShawn brought the dollar his mother gave him each Sunday for Sunday school. But Deka gladly brought the $9.50 she had earned during the week. Deka was so excited about her gift, she couldn't wait to get to Sunday school.

The Bible says, "God loves a cheerful giver." He doesn't want us to give because we have to. He wants us to give because we *want* to. God says that when we want to give to others, He will help us find ways to do that. And the more we give, the more He will give to us. Isn't that amazing?

Let's talk: Why wasn't DeShawn a cheerful giver? What kind of giver does God want us to be? Why did Deka want extra chores? How did God bless Deka? Who do you think was happier—DeShawn or Deka? Why?

Older children and adults may read: 2 Corinthians 9:6–8

Let's pray: Dear God, we thank You for the many gifts You give us every day. We thank You especially for Jesus and His love. Make us willing and cheerful givers so that we will gladly share with others the things You have given us. In Jesus' name we ask this. Amen.

[Jesus said,] "If two of you on earth agree about anything you ask for, it will be done for you by My Father in heaven. Matthew 18:19

Praying Together Helps

"Lissa, you ask Daddy to have a picnic tomorrow," said her brother, Brett.

"No, you ask him," replied Lissa.

"Let's both ask him," said Brett.

So they both asked their daddy to have a picnic. When he saw that both children wanted to have a picnic, he said, "Well, if you both want it, maybe we can." Lissa and Brett were excited.

We can talk that way to God our Father too. When you ask God for something, He hears you, and when your friends or parents talk to God, He hears them too. But there are some things that many Christians want. If we pray together about those things, even if there are only two of us, Jesus says that God will listen and answer our prayer.

What are some things we all want? We want to be loved, we want to be happy, we want to be more like Jesus, we want other people to learn about Him! Let's pray for those things together, and our Father in heaven will hear our prayer and answer us.

Are there other things that you want? Jesus said, "If two of you on earth agree about anything you ask for, it will be done for you by My Father in heaven." Isn't that a wonderful promise? Next time you have a special request for God, ask someone to pray about it with you and see what happens!

Let's talk: Why did Lissa and Brett both ask their daddy to go on a picnic? What did Jesus say would happen when two of His friends asked His Father for something? What are some things nearly all Christians want? What are some things you want?

Older children and adults may read: Matthew 18:19–20

Let's pray: Thank You, dear Father in heaven, for promising to hear Your children's prayers and do what You know is best for us. We want what Jesus wants, so please make us more like Him. Please keep us as Your children for Jesus' sake. Amen.

Dorcas… was always doing good. Acts 9:36

Are We Full of Good Works?

Dorcas was dead, and many people were crying. Most of them were widows. Widows are women whose husbands have died. Most of the widows had children to feed. Dorcas had helped them. She had made dresses and coats for them. That's why they loved her. But now she was dead.

Some of her friends told Peter that Dorcas was dead. Peter was one of Jesus' 12 disciples. Peter went to Dorcas' house and asked Jesus to make Dorcas alive again.

Jesus answered Peter's prayer. He made Dorcas alive and well again. When she opened her eyes and saw Peter, she sat up. Dorcas' friends were very happy when they saw her alive, especially the widows whom she had helped. "She was always doing good," they said. Wouldn't we like to have people say that about us?

How did Dorcas get to be full of good works? She loved and believed in Jesus. Because she had Jesus living in her heart, she showed her love for Him by doing nice things for others. Maybe the first day nobody noticed. And maybe not on the second day either. But soon everybody noticed that Dorcas was helping people. That's why they said, "She was always doing good."

Can people say that we are full of good works? That depends on whether we treat others the way we want to be treated. How kind and helpful are we? Jesus, who lives in our hearts, too, wants us to always do good things. And today is the best time to start doing them. Jesus will help you see the ways you can help others.

Let's talk: What happened to Dorcas? Why were the people sad? Whom did they tell? What did Peter do? What did the people say about Dorcas? Who helped her "always do good"? How do we become full of good works? When is a good time to start helping other people?

Older children and adults may read: Acts 9:36–42

Let's pray: Dear Father in heaven, You have been so good to us. We thank You especially for sending Jesus to save us. Please teach us to do what we can for other people. Show us how to start doing good in our own home and with our friends and neighbors. We want to "always do good" just like Dorcas. We ask this for Jesus' sake, our Lord and Savior. Amen.

[Jesus said,] "Take heart." Matthew 9:2

How Cheerful Are You?

Everybody in the hospital called her Grandma Sunshine. She was in the hospital because she had fallen down some steps and broken her back. The big cast on her body had to stay on for a long time. But every time someone came to visit her or check on her, Grandma Sunshine smiled and said, "Cheer up." She was a cheerful person.

There was another lady in Grandma Sunshine's room. The doctors didn't know what was wrong with her, so she was in the hospital for some tests. She was going home in a few days, but she spent the whole time worrying and complaining. She didn't like the room, the bed was too hard, the food wasn't any good, and the nurses weren't nice. The nurses called her Miss Grumpy.

Why was Grandma Sunshine always smiling, even though her back hurt? Why didn't she complain about being in the hospital for so long? Because Grandma Sunshine knew she was one of God's dear children. She was also thankful for what the hospital people did for her.

Children and adults often grumble and complain instead of being cheerful. But Jesus gives us a reason for being happy, even when we are sick. "Take heart," He said to a crippled man whose friends had brought him to Jesus.

Do you know why we can be happy, no matter what happens to us? Jesus told the crippled man, "Your sins are forgiven." That's the main reason we can be happy. Our sins are forgiven because Jesus paid for them on the cross. So "take heart." Be cheerful. God loves us and has forgiven us.

Let's talk: What did people call the lady with the broken back? Why? How did Grandma Sunshine's roommate show that she wasn't happy? Why was Grandma Sunshine always ready to smile? What did Jesus tell the crippled man? What's the best reason for being cheerful all the time?

Older children and adults may read: Matthew 9:1–7

Let's pray: Dear Jesus, how glad we are that You forgive all our sins and that You are our God. Help us remember this so that we will be cheerful even when things don't go our way. In Your name. Amen.

[Simon Peter said,] "You have the words of eternal life."
John 6:68

Our Heavenly Map

When people take a long trip, they often take a map. Do you know why? They want to know what roads will get them where they want to go. The map directs them. It shows them the way.

We all want to get to heaven. But not everybody knows the way. In the story "This Way to Heaven," Jimmy Wheeler asked a man standing by a church door, "Mister, is this the way to heaven?"

In church, we learn that the way to heaven is Jesus. We learn this from the Bible. The Bible is like a map. The Bible says that Jesus is the only Way to heaven. All who follow Him are on the right road. Jesus is the road that takes us to heaven.

A map not only shows the way to get somewhere, it also shows what we will see along the way. It shows the towns we will pass through and the bridges we need to cross and the mountains and lakes we will see. A good map also shows the detours we need to take so we won't get lost or turn off on the wrong road.

In all these ways, the Bible is like a map. Through it, Jesus directs our way so that we won't get lost. That's why we need to study our Bible. It tells us how to follow Jesus to heaven. His words are the words of eternal life.

Let's talk: What does a driver often take on a long trip? Why? In what way is the Bible like a map? Who does the Bible say is the only way to heaven? What did Peter say to Jesus in our Bible verse? Where can we find the words of Jesus? How will studying the Bible help us along the way to heaven?

Older children and adults may read: John 6:62–69

Let's pray: Dear Jesus, we're thankful that we have learned that You are the Way to heaven. Keep us close to You on the way so that we won't get lost on the wrong roads. We ask this as Your dear children. Amen.

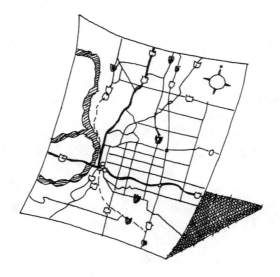

Tomorrow will worry about itself. Matthew 6:34

Don't Worry about Tomorrow

One evening Martin Luther looked out a window in his house. In a tree nearby, he saw a little bird getting ready for the night. Look how that little bird teaches us to trust in God, Luther said to himself. That bird takes hold of his twig, tucks his head under his wing, and goes to sleep. He lets God care for him.

Even children often worry about tomorrow. They wonder what they'll get to do, or whether they'll have good grades in school, or how they can become somebody's best friend, or what people will think about them.

Jesus once told us to look at the birds. They don't worry about tomorrow. They don't even work, and God still feeds them. "Are you not much more valuable than they?" Jesus asked.

Jesus wants people to work. The Bible says, "If a man will not work, he shall not eat." God wants children to learn how to work. But He tells us not to worry about our work or about anything else. He loves us and will take care of us. We can trust in Him.

"Only believe," said Jesus to a man who was worried that his daughter was dead. Jesus made the girl alive. All we have to do is trust in Jesus, and He will see that everything turns out for the best.

Let's talk: What did Martin Luther see outside his window one evening? How did the little bird go to sleep? What do you sometimes worry about? What do adults sometimes worry about? Why did Jesus tell us not to worry about food and clothes? How do we know that He wants us to work, even though He doesn't want us to worry? What did Jesus tell Jairus when his daughter died?

Older children and adults may read: Matthew 6:24–34

Let's pray: Dear Lord Jesus, help us trust in You so that we don't have to worry. Teach us that tomorrow will take care of itself because You are our God and care for us. In Your name. Amen.

Seek and you will find. Matthew 7:7

Pray and Work

Did you ever watch a chicken hunt for something to eat? It often stands and scratches the ground. It scratches the grass and stones away. When it sees something to eat, it picks it up. Chickens scratch for a living.

God has promised to bless us, and He gives us the ability to work for what we want. We ask God for daily bread, and He gives us jobs to earn money to buy food.

When Jesus talked about God's blessings, He told us to go after them. "Seek and you will find," He said. We are to ask God for the things we need, and look and listen for the ways He gives them to us.

When we ask God to teach us more about Himself, His answer is in the Bible. He tells us, "Seek and you will find." Then we learn about His Word in Sunday school and church. With our family, we learn stories and Bible verses about Jesus. That's where we find God's promises.

‿

Let's talk: Why does Jesus tell us to "seek and you will find"? What if we seek something that God doesn't want us to have? Why will God always help us find what's best for us? Where can we find God's promises of love and forgiveness?

Older children and adults may read: Matthew 13:45–46

Let's pray: Dear Father in heaven, thank You for the promise that we will find Your blessings when we look for them and depend on You to provide them. Lead us to ask for those things that You want us to have. This we ask in Jesus' name. Amen.

Rejoice in the Lord always. Philippians 4:4

A Boy Who Was Always Happy

A woman pushed a wheelchair down the sidewalk. A young boy sat in the wheelchair. He couldn't walk. He couldn't even move his hands very well. He had multiple sclerosis. But he was smiling as the woman pushed him down the street.

"Look at that boy. Look at the big smile on his face," said Gregory.

"I'd cry if I couldn't walk," said his sister, Mia.

"That boy is doing what Jesus wants us all to do, though," said Gregory. "Don't you remember what our minister said about being happy all the time? 'Rejoice in the Lord always.' That's a Bible verse."

"But how can I rejoice if I don't feel happy?" asked Mia. She sounded as though she were about to cry.

"We can remember how Jesus was nailed on the cross for us," said Gregory. "That shows how much He loves us. And because He loves us so much, we can be happy no matter what problems we might have. Jesus even makes people happy when they can't walk."

"I guess you're right," said Mia. "But since we can run and play, we should *really* be happy and rejoice."

Gregory and Mia both rejoiced in the Lord. The next day they went and introduced themselves to the boy in the wheelchair. They wanted to tell him how he had helped them rejoice.

Let's talk: How did the boy in the wheelchair show that he was happy? Do you think you could smile if you weren't able to walk? What are some good things you would still have? What does the Bible verse tell us? Because we belong to Jesus, why can we always rejoice?

Older children and adults may read: Philippians 4:4–7

Let's pray: Dear God, thank You for the bodies and legs You have given us and for all Your other blessings. We thank You most of all for loving us and making us Your children. Help us to be happy always here on earth because we know You are going to take us to heaven. We ask this in Jesus' name. Amen.

[Peter] said, "Lord, You know all things." John 21:17

Jesus Knows Everything

One day Jesus asked Peter, "Do you love Me?" Three times Jesus asked him this question. The third time Peter said, "Lord, You know all things; You know that I love You." Jesus did know that Peter loved Him. He knows everything. Isn't that wonderful?

It can be scary too. If Jesus knows everything, He knows all the bad things we think too.

Mandy didn't like her teacher. *I hope Mr. Donner dies soon. Then I can have a new teacher,* Mandy thought. She would never say something like that out loud, but she was thinking it. People around her didn't know what she was thinking, but Jesus knew.

Jesus knows everything. He knows the bad things we say and do and even those we only think. He knows all about us, but He still loves us. He forgives all our sins because He loves us. He even suffered and died on the cross to save us from being punished for what we do wrong.

And Jesus knows that we really love Him, even when our actions don't show that we do. Deron wanted to make Jesus happy, so he tried to be kind to his little brother. He reached into the cabinet to get a glass so that he could get his little brother a drink. The glass fell and broke, and his mother got angry. She didn't know why Jimmy had broken the glass, but Jesus knew.

We are glad Jesus knows everything.

Let's talk: What question did Jesus ask Peter three times? What did Peter say the third time? Why is that a scary thought? Would we want our minister to know everything we think? Why is God always happy to forgive our sins? Why can we be glad that Jesus knows everything? Memorize the Bible verse.

Older children and adults may read: John 21:14–17

Let's pray: Dear Lord, please forgive us for not always showing that we love You. Help us to think and talk and act the way You want us to. We love You and want to love You more. In Jesus' name. Amen.

How great is the love the Father has lavished on us, that we should be called children of God! 1 John 3:1

Adopted Children of God

Jamie's parents were often drunk, which meant they didn't take very good care of her. When she was still a tiny baby, some neighbors heard her crying and called the police. Jamie was alone in the house and very hungry.

The police found Jamie's parents in a bar. They were arrested and had to appear in court before a judge. The judge told Jamie's parents that there was a family willing to adopt their baby. Her parents gave Jamie to the judge so he could put her in a new home.

For a long time Jamie's new parents were afraid to tell her that she was adopted. They thought she wouldn't love them as much if she knew they weren't her real parents. But one day Jamie found out. Some children at school told her that the people she thought were her parents weren't her *real* parents. Jamie thought about the news all day.

That evening Jamie talked to her father. "You love me a lot, don't you?" she asked.

"We love you very much," said Father. "But why are you asking? Don't you know how much we love you?"

"I was just wondering. You made me your daughter even though I really wasn't your daughter," Jamie explained. "You didn't have to do that."

Jamie was right. Parents love their adopted children as much as they would love their natural children. One day the disciple John thought about how God had adopted us as His children. God didn't have to do that. John said, "How great is the love the Father has lavished on us, that we should be called children of God!"

The Bible says, "You are all sons of God through faith in Christ Jesus." Because Jesus is our Savior, God has adopted us and calls us His children. He does this for Jesus' sake. Think of how much God loves us! Think of how wonderful it is to be one of His dear children!

Let's talk: Whose daughter did Jamie become when she was adopted? Why did her new parents adopt Jamie? What did Jamie say when she found out that she was adopted? Whom does God adopt as His children? Why is God eager to make us His children? How do you feel about this?

Older children and adults may read: 1 John 3:1–3

Let's pray: Dear Father in heaven, how glad we are that You have adopted us. How much You must love us! Keep us as Your children, and help us show our thanks through our actions. We ask this for Jesus' sake. Amen.

I will fear no evil, for You are with me. Psalm 23:4

How to Be Brave

Carlos and Jake were reading about Elijah and how he was taken into heaven in a chariot of fire. The two boys talked about the chariot and how it must have looked. They wondered about the horses that pulled it.

"I'd be afraid to ride in a chariot like that, wouldn't you?" asked Carlos.

"I wouldn't be afraid—at least not if God were driving," Jake answered.

People who believe in Jesus know that God loves them. They say what King David said in Psalm 23, "The Lord is my Shepherd." Jesus is like a good shepherd who takes very good care of his lambs and sheep. Jesus doesn't let anything hurt us.

Do you know the rest of Psalm 23? In it, King David also said, "I will fear no evil, for You are with me." People who belong to Jesus have the promise that He will hold them close. Then they can always be brave. They don't need to be afraid. The Bible says that everything turns out good for those who love Jesus.

We don't ever have to be afraid because we know that Jesus will always take care of us. Remembering that Jesus is with us all the time and loves us very much makes us brave and happy. He even died on the cross for us. Don't ever forget that.

Let's talk: Why is Jesus called the Good Shepherd? Who are His lambs and sheep? How do we know Jesus is always near us? Why can we be brave when we belong to Jesus? Memorize the Bible verse.

Older children and adults may read: Psalm 23

Let's pray: Dear Lord Jesus, our Savior and Good Shepherd, we know that You are with us and that we belong to You. Help us remember this every day so that we won't fear anything. Make us brave and happy, like David, and keep us close to You always. In Your name. Amen.

Be joyful always. 1 Thessalonians 5:16

When to Be Happy

Melinda had to wear braces on her legs to walk. She had multiple sclerosis. Even though she couldn't walk very well, she went to school with all her friends.

One day Melinda fell down the stairs at school. Her teacher was afraid that Melinda had been badly hurt. Mr. Blythe ran to Melinda and asked, "Are you hurt?"

Melinda smiled and said, "No, I've learned how to fall."

Melinda had learned how to be happy even when things didn't go right. She could smile even when she fell or hurt herself. In our Bible verse, God tells us to be joyful all the time. No matter what happens to us, we can be happy when we remember how much God loves us.

Can you smile, even when things don't go your way? When things go wrong, remember how much Jesus loves you. He will help you be happy.

Let's talk: Can people be happy even when they have to wear braces on their legs? What's the best reason we have for being happy? How do we know that God loves us? How do we want to act because we're God's children? Memorize the Bible verse.

Older children and adults may read: 1 Thessalonians 5:14–23

Let's pray: Dear God, we're glad that Jesus made us Your children. Forgive us for not always being happy. Help us smile even when things aren't going right. We know that You love us and that's reason enough for us to be happy always. Amen.

In Christ God forgave you. Ephesians 4:32

Why Our Sins Are Forgiven

Tadashi looked at a picture book of India. There was a huge, fat idol on one page. People were bowing down to it. Others were lighting sticks for it, and some were giving it food and money.

"Mom, why are they doing that?" Tadashi asked.

"Because they want the idol to forgive their sins and give them blessings," his mom told him.

"We don't have to do that to have our sins forgiven, do we?" asked Tadashi. "We don't have to burn candles or pay God for what we do wrong, do we?"

"No, God is much better to us than that idol is to people," Mom answered. "We don't need to pay anything to have our sins forgiven. But somebody did have to pay for them."

"I know," said Tadashi. "Jesus paid for our sins."

"I'm glad you know that, Tadashi," said Mom. "And we love Jesus for having done that, don't we?"

"Yeah, and for letting us know about it so we don't have to pay a fat idol," Tadashi said with a smile. "That idol couldn't forgive us anyhow."

Let's talk: What were the people in the picture giving to an idol? Why do people give presents to idols? Who has paid for everyone's sins? How did Jesus pay for our sins? For whose sake does God forgive us? How do we show our thanks?

Older children and adults may read: Psalm 85

Let's pray: Thank You, dear heavenly Father, for loving and forgiving us. Help the missionaries who preach the good news about Jesus to people. Help people all over the world to know that Jesus is their Savior. We ask this in Jesus' name. Amen.

Love your neighbor as yourself. Romans 13:9

The Golden Rule

Alicia ran into the house to tell her mother what her brother was doing. "Charlie pushed me. And then he threw my doll on the ground. And now he won't let me swing," she said. She wanted her mother to get mad at Charlie.

One day Alicia's mother took a sheet of paper and drew a line down the center. "First tell me all the things you want Charlie to do," Mother said. Alicia told her many things, and her mother wrote them on one side of the paper.

"I want him to let me swing. And I want him to let me go to the store with him. And I want to play with his soccer ball. And I want him to read me the comics. And I *don't* want him to hit me," Alicia said. And she took a big breath and went on and on.

When she was finally finished, Mother asked Alicia to tell her the things she wanted to do *for* Charlie. At first Alicia couldn't think of anything.

"The Bible says, 'Love your neighbor as yourself,' " Mother said. "God wants us to love other people just as much as we love ourselves. We don't want others to hurt us, so we won't want to hurt them. And if we want others to be kind to us, we will be kind to them."

Then Alicia and her mother began to list what Alicia could do for her brother. When the lists on both sides were the same length, Mother said, "Remember that Jesus wants you to love Charlie the way you want Charlie to love you."

After that list, Alicia and Charlie played together much better.

~

Let's talk: Why do you think Alicia was a tattletale? What are some things you like to have people do for you? Do you ever like it when someone hurts or says mean things about you? What is the Golden Rule? Who is our neighbor?

Older children and adults may read: Romans 13:8–10

Let's pray: Thank You, dear Jesus, for loving us more than You loved Yourself. Help us show our love for You by loving others the way we love ourselves. In Your name. Amen.

Do not forget to do good and to share with others.
Hebrews 13:16

Something to Remember

Wesley received $10 from his uncle for his birthday. He also got a video game from his parents and a football from his neighbors. It was fun having a birthday and getting presents.

The next day was Devon's birthday. Devon lived down the street, but his family didn't have much money. Wesley took his $10 and bought Devon three comic books. Wesley knew that Devon loved comic books.

Devon's eyes popped wide open when he saw the present. "Wow! Thanks, thanks a whole lot!" he said. Then Wesley knew it was true. It's more fun to give than to receive.

The prophet Elijah once visited a widow. The widow had only a little food left. After that was gone, she thought she would die. Elijah asked the widow for something to eat. He told her that God would give her enough flour and oil to feed herself, her son, and Elijah.

Elijah's request was a test for the widow. She gave Elijah some food because she believed what he had said about God's promise. And God kept His promise and gave her enough food for her family.

The Bible says, "Do not forget to do good." In another place, it says we should take every opportunity to do good to others. God is pleased when we do helpful things.

Let's talk: Was Wesley happy when he received his birthday gifts? What made him feel even better? How did God bless the widow who gave food to His servant Elijah? What does the Bible tell us not to forget? How often are we to treat others well? Why do we want to do good things?

Older children and adults may read: 1 Timothy 6:17–19

Let's pray: Dear heavenly Father, You give us so much every day. Please forgive us for being selfish. Make us willing to do what we can for others. In Jesus' name we pray. Amen.

The Son of Man has authority on earth to forgive sins.
Matthew 9:6

The Load Only Jesus Can Lift

"Wow! Isn't he strong!" said the people as they watched the strong man in the circus. The strong man asked two men from the audience to come and lift one of his weights. They couldn't lift it. Then he took one weight in one hand and another in the other hand. He lifted them both high above his head.

But there is a load that the strong man can't lift. The load is sin. The only one who can lift it is Jesus.

One day a sick man was brought to Jesus. His friends wanted to help him get well. But Jesus wanted to do something else first. He wanted to forgive the man's sins. This man's sins were like a heavy load. So when Jesus saw him and the faith he and his friends had, Jesus said, "Your sins are forgiven." And to show that He had the power to forgive sins, Jesus told the man, "Pick up your bed and walk." Right away the sick man could do it.

Did you ever notice that when you have done something bad, you don't feel very good? It bothers you and keeps bothering you. It's like a heavy load. But when you tell your parents or friends that you're sorry, and you ask Jesus to forgive you, then you feel good again. The load is gone.

Jesus forgives sins. He paid for all sins by dying on the cross. That's why the Bible says that Jesus has the power to forgive sins.

Let's talk: Why did the friends bring the sick man to Jesus? What did Jesus say to the man? How did Jesus show that He has the power to forgive sins? How can we get rid of our sins? Memorize the Bible verse.

Older children and adults may read: Matthew 9:1–8

Let's pray: Dear Lord Jesus, please forgive all the wrong things we have done. Don't let our sins bother us like a heavy load. Take them all away. We know You can because You are God's Son and have the power to forgive sins. Thank You, dear Jesus, for loving us. Amen.

You will see the Son of Man ... coming on the clouds of heaven. Matthew 26:64

The Biggest Surprise Ever

"Will that ever be a surprise!" said Kristen as she came home from church.

"What will be a surprise?" asked Dad. He had stayed home and was reading the comics.

"It'll be a big surprise when all the people of the world see Jesus coming on the clouds of heaven," Kristen explained. "Jesus said He would. He said it when He was standing in front of Caiaphas."

Kristen's dad didn't believe her, but Kristen was right. Caiaphas didn't like Jesus. He wanted to kill Jesus. He asked Jesus, "Are You the Savior God promised to send?"

Jesus answered, "Yes, it is as you say. In the future you will see Me coming on the clouds of heaven."

Caiaphas didn't believe Jesus either. Lots of people don't believe that Jesus is coming again. But Jesus said He will return, and everybody will see Him coming. We'll see Him coming in the clouds too.

Because Jesus is our Savior, we're glad He's coming back. When He comes again, He will take us to live with Him in heaven. That will be like all the Christmases and birthdays and Easters and every other fun party we've ever had—even better. It will be the most wonderful day ever. That's why Kristen was happy.

~

Let's talk: Who is going to come again? Why will this be a surprise? How will Caiaphas feel when he sees Jesus coming? Who else will see Jesus coming? How will the people who believe in Jesus feel? What will happen to them?

Older children and adults may read: Luke 21:25–36

Let's pray: Dear Lord Jesus, we're glad that You are coming again. We know that You will take us to heaven. Please help us tell everyone we can about You so that they can believe in You and not be surprised when You come. Amen.

Blessed are all who take refuge in Him. Psalm 2:12

We Trust in Jesus

Keith and his dad were walking in the woods. They came to a small river that didn't have a bridge. Someone had put a long log across the water in order to cross the river.

Keith was afraid to walk on the log. He was afraid he would fall into the water. But when Dad said, "I'll carry you across," Keith wasn't afraid anymore. He trusted his dad.

We can trust Jesus just like Keith trusted his dad. Jesus is the Son of God and can do anything. He's the Ruler of the world and can help us in any trouble.

When Keith's dad carried him across the river, Keith still hung on for dear life. He was both glad and scared. He was glad to have his dad's strong and loving arms around him, but he was a little scared and held on tightly.

Like Keith, we need to hold on to Jesus so that we won't slip away from Him. Our Bible verse says, "Blessed are all who take refuge in Him." This means we can be happy and safe in Jesus' loving arms because He will carry us across dangers all the way to heaven.

⁓

Let's talk: What was Keith afraid to do by himself? When was Keith not afraid to cross the river? What does it mean to trust someone? How did Keith trust his father? Why can we trust Jesus to help and save us? What does the Bible verse say about all who put their trust in Jesus?

Older children and adults may read: Psalm 46

Let's pray: Dear Lord Jesus, hold us close to You in Your strong and loving arms every day. Then we know that we are safe and will get where You want us to go. We love You. Amen.

Faith comes from hearing ... the word of Christ.
Romans 10:17

How People Become Christians

Chief Kawa took his bow and arrows. He walked quietly to some bushes behind the place where a missionary was talking.

Nobody saw Kawa. He didn't want to be seen. But while Kawa got ready to shoot the man, he heard him tell a story. It was the story of a lost lamb. "God is like a shepherd," the missionary said. "He loves His sheep. He does not want to lose any. So He sent His Son, Jesus, to save His sheep."

When Kawa heard those words, he didn't try to harm the missionary. He hid his bow and arrows in the bushes and listened. When the sermon was over, Kawa went to the missionary. "Tell me more about Jesus," he said. Kawa became a Christian. He believed that Jesus was his Savior, and he loved Him. Kawa lived his life for Jesus.

How did all this happen? It happened when Kawa heard some preaching. If Kawa hadn't heard about Jesus, he would never have loved Him. By hearing the Word of God, the Holy Spirit could put faith in Jesus in his heart. Kawa loved Jesus and wanted to be one of His people. That is what faith means.

To get faith we must hear and learn the Word of God. "Faith comes from hearing ... the word of Christ." When we give money at church, we can help send missionaries so that people everywhere can hear God's Word and learn about Jesus, their Savior.

Let's talk: What did Kawa want to do? Why didn't he hurt the missionary? How did Kawa become a Christian? What does it mean to believe in Jesus? How did we get our faith? Why are we glad to help missionaries?

Older children and adults may read: Romans 10:14–17

Let's pray: Dear Father in heaven, we're glad that we can hear and learn Your words in the Bible. Give us a strong faith in Jesus and all that You have said. Bless all preaching and teaching of Your Word so that many more people will hear and learn about Jesus. We ask this in Jesus' name. Amen.

Praise the Lord your God for the good land He has given you.
Deuteronomy 8:10

The Refugee Family

"Dad, what are refugees?" asked Neal. A refugee family had moved into the house next door.

"Refugees are people who had to leave their homes in a faraway land," answered Dad.

"Why did they have to leave their homes? Did they do something bad?" asked Neal.

"No, there was a war, and some enemies took their homes," Dad explained.

"People in our country are safe, aren't they?" said Neal.

"Yes, as long as God protects us. He has been good to the people in our country," Dad said. "Most of us have a home, and most people have jobs, and most have enough to eat.

"Do you know what Moses told the people of Israel to do when God gave them a home in the good country of Canaan?" Dad asked.

Neal shook his head no.

" 'Praise the Lord your God for the good land He has given you,' Moses told the Israelites," Dad said. "Moses knew that there were plenty of good things in the land of Canaan."

"You know, in some countries the children have to go to bed hungry every day because they don't get enough to eat," Neal said. He had heard this in Sunday school.

"That's right," said his father. "And that's not the only reason why we do what the Bible verse says. Can you think of another?"

Neal thought for a while. "I know," he said. "In our country, we can have our own church, and we can go when we want to."

"That's right," said Dad. "And that's one of the best reasons for thanking God for our country."

~

Let's talk: Why did the refugees leave their home in a faraway country? Why do some people in other countries go to bed hungry? In what ways is God good to us and the people in our country? Memorize the Bible verse.

Older children and adults may read: Deuteronomy 8:5–20

Let's pray: We praise and thank You, God, for the good land You have given us. Help us show our thanks by gladly obeying Your commands. In Jesus' name we ask this. Amen.

It is good to praise the Lord. Psalm 92:1

Giving God Thanks

A Sunday school class made up a litany. A litany is a prayer in which one person says the first part of a sentence and all the others say the second part. This one was a prayer of thanks and praise. It went like this:

For sending Jesus to be our Savior,
Dear God, we thank and praise You.

For the Holy Bible,
Dear God, we thank and praise You.

For parents who teach us about Jesus and His love,
Dear God, we thank and praise You.

For our church and church school,
Dear God, we thank and praise You.

For making us Your children,
Dear God, we thank and praise You.

For our family and our home,
Dear God, we thank and praise You.

For Your love and care and blessings,
Dear God, we thank and praise You.

The Bible says, "It is good to praise the Lord." It is good because He deserves to be thanked and praised for the kindness He shows us every day. It is also good for us. It makes us happy when we think of how good God is to us and when we praise and thank Him.

We thank and praise God when we pray and when we sing—at home and in church. Of course, we can thank Him without speaking. But what if we could not speak or sing to God at all? How sad we would be! "It is good to praise the Lord." So let's do it often, alone and together, at home and at church.

Let's talk: What are some things for which God deserves to be thanked and praised? What does our Bible verse say about giving praise to the Lord? Why is it good for us to give thanks and praise to the Lord?

Older children and adults may read: Psalm 92:1–5

Let's pray: Dear God, we want to thank and praise You for all that You have done for us. You created this beautiful world. You sent Jesus to die for us on the cross. And you love us as Your children. How good You are to all of us, dear Lord. Help us show our love for You every day, for Jesus' sake. Amen.

Freely you have received, freely give. Matthew 10:8

God's Gifts Are Free

Once a rosebush and a snail lived together in the corner of a garden. The rosebush was happy all day long. It was thankful that God gave it fresh air and warm sun and good rain. Every day it grew a little more, and soon it was covered with roses. The sweet, beautiful flowers praised God and made people happy.

The snail lived underneath the rosebush. It liked to stay in the shadows and do nothing. When anyone came near, it crawled into its shell as if to say, "I'm not interested in anybody else."

One day the snail said to the rosebush, "You're foolish for always giving people your roses." The rosebush smiled back and said, "How can I help giving away the things God gives to me?"

God's children are always receiving His gifts of love free of charge. Every day we receive His forgiveness and His Spirit. We also receive His loving care and our daily food. Why shouldn't we gladly share God's gifts with others, especially the sweet story of Jesus and what He has done for the whole world?

Jesus said, "Freely you have received, freely give." Let us gladly give to other people what we receive freely from God. Then we will be more like a rose than a snail.

Let's talk: What do rosebushes give people? Who gives roses to the rosebushes? Why does God want us to be like a rosebush and not like a snail? What are some of the things God gives us every day without making us pay? What's the best gift God gives to us all the time? How can we give this gift to others?

Older children and adults may read: Luke 6:30–38

Let's pray: Dear Jesus, we thank You for giving us Your love and blessings freely every day. Help us share them by giving them freely to others. Amen.

Today in the town of David a Savior has been born to you;
He is Christ the Lord. Luke 2:11

The Most Wonderful Night

Everything was dark, but the shepherds watching their sheep near Bethlehem were used to that. Many nights had been dark and lonely for them, and they didn't expect this night to be any different. They didn't know that their nights would never have to be lonely again.

Suddenly there was a bright light around them. The glory of God was shining down on them. At first the shepherds were terribly afraid of what might happen. Then they heard an angel talk to them. The angel said, "Do not be afraid. I bring you good news that will make you very happy. For you a little baby has just been born over there in Bethlehem. He is the Lord, the promised Savior. You will find the baby lying in a manger, wrapped in strips of cloth."

Then many more angels came and still more, until there were more than anybody could count. They were all praising God and singing. "Glory to God in the highest, and on earth peace to men on whom His favor rests," they sang.

When the angels had gone back to heaven, the shepherds said to one another, "Let us go to Bethlehem right away and see the Savior." So they left their sheep and hurried away. In Bethlehem they found Mary and Joseph, and the baby Jesus lying on some hay in a manger. How happy they were! What the angel had told them was true! God's Son, the promised Savior, had come from heaven to save them from their sins and take them to heaven. The shepherds left the manger and told many others what they knew about Jesus.

Let's talk: What is the night called on which Jesus was born? Who were the first ones to hear about the coming of Jesus? How did God tell the shepherds that their Savior had come? Why did the angels sing? Where did the shepherds find Jesus? What did the shepherds do after they had seen the baby Jesus? Why are all Christians glad that Jesus came?

Older children and adults may read: Luke 2:8–20

Let's pray:
>Be near me, Lord Jesus, I ask Thee to stay
>>Close by me forever and love me, I pray.
>Bless all the dear children in Thy tender care,
>>And take us to heaven to live with Thee there.
>Amen.

≈

He has risen, just as He said. Matthew 28:6

The Most Wonderful Day

Jesus lived on earth a long time ago, as you know. After He grew up, He went from one place to the next and told people that He was God's Son. Jesus taught them about heaven and about how they could become God's children. He said that He had come to save all people from their sins.

Wherever He went, many people followed Jesus. They wanted to learn more about Him and His Father in heaven. They also brought their children and their sick friends to Jesus. He loved and helped them. After a while they wanted to make Him their king.

But the church leaders didn't love Jesus. They didn't believe that He was the Savior God had promised to send. So they arrested Him and hung Him on the cross to die. The Bible tells us that Jesus let them do this to Him. He was willing to die so that the sins of everyone in the world could be forgiven.

Three days after Jesus was killed, the most wonderful thing happened. It was early in the morning. Soldiers were guarding Jesus' grave. All at once the earth shook. A shining angel came down from heaven and rolled the stone away from the door of Jesus' grave. The soldiers fell over like dead men. When they got up, the angel and Jesus were gone.

Early that morning some women who loved Jesus came to His grave. Mary Magdalene was one of them. When the women saw that the grave was open, Mary Magdalene ran back to the city to tell the disciples. The other women went into the grave. Inside, they saw two angels. One of them said, "We know you are looking for Jesus. He isn't here. He's risen!" The women hurried to Jerusalem to tell the disciples what they had seen and heard.

A little later Mary Magdalene came back to the grave alone. She was crying because she thought someone had stolen Jesus' body. Suddenly, Jesus stood near her. Mary thought He was a gardener. "Sir," she said, "if you have taken Jesus away, tell me where you have put Him."

Jesus said, "Mary!" Then she knew it was Jesus. Jesus told her to tell His disciples that He was alive. Mary was so happy. She ran to tell her friends the good news.

Let's talk: Why did people want Jesus to be their king? Why did Jesus have to die? What happened on the first Easter morning? What did the angel tell the women? How did Mary Magdalene know that Jesus really was alive?

Older children and adults may read: Matthew 28:1–8

Let's pray: Dear Lord Jesus, please fill our hearts with Easter joy. Help us all to believe that You are our living Savior. Live in our hearts so that we will live with You now and forever in heaven. Amen.

Scripture Index